The Intellectual and the Marketplace

The
INTELLECTUAL
and the
MARKETPLACE

Enlarged Edition

George J. Stigler

Harvard University Press
Cambridge, Massachusetts
and London, England
1984

Copyright © 1984 by the President and Fellows of Harvard College
Copyright © 1963 by George J. Stigler
All rights reserved
Printed in the United States of America
10 9 8 7 6 5 4 3 2 1

This book is printed on acid-free paper, and its binding materials have
been chosen for strength and durability.

Library of Congress Cataloging in Publication Data

Stigler, George Joseph, 1911–
The intellectual and the marketplace.

Bibliography: p.
Includes index.
1. Economics—Anecdotes, facetiae, satire, etc.
2. Education, Higher—Anecdotes, facetiae, satire, etc.   I. Title.
HB171.S875   1984   330   84-6654
ISBN 0-674-45735-8
ISBN 0-674-45736-6 (pbk.)

Preface

My old friend Adam Smith has told me that a "disposition for mirth often takes away from the force of . . . orations . . . , and indeed is not at all fitted for raising any of the passions which are chiefly to be excited by oratory, viz. Compassion and indignation." I feebly pray that just this once he is half wrong, for I hope to excite your compassion for sundry causes, and yet employ the weapon of mirth.

Contents

_____TWO_____
All about Economics

ONE

Mostly about Universities

1

An Academic Episode

I had been proposing a favorite thesis: that our universities are run in reverse. While a man is still young and energetic and curious, he is required to teach so many elementary courses and read so many examinations—and scrub so many floors at home—that he can do no research. Even his summers must be spent earning more money. When he gets older, his teaching load is cut in half and his paperwork is delegated to assistants—and his salary doubles. But by then he is usually beyond creative work, and develops his bridge game or gardening skills. Pinzio, the venerable head of Romance Languages, agreed that there was much truth in the indictment, but thought that any remedy would be worse than the disease. He related the following story.

About thirty years ago a young man named Seguira became the rector of a university in a South American country in which his father had recently financed a successful revolution. Seguira, who previously had been quite the gay young blade, surprised everyone when he immediately settled down to become a serious-minded reformer—a sort of Latin Hutchins. He began casting about for reform, of which—Pinzio said—the university could stand a good deal, and eventually hit upon the merit system. He soon issued the following regulations.

In June of each year any member of the faculty could challenge the person immediately above him a rank to a competitive examination. The examination was to be made up and graded by a group of impartial professors in the United States. (Seguira told Pinzio that this country had been chosen in order to make bribery more expensive.) If the challenger won, he would exchange position and salary with his former superior. Thus an able graduate student could in successive years become an instructor, an assistant professor, an associate professor, and a professor.

There was a terrible uproar, and some shrill glee, when this announcement came out. Some of the older men were very bitter, and emphasized the fact that the rectorship was not included in the competition. But most of the younger members of the faculty were delighted at the prospect, Pinzio among them.

The announcement was made in September, and some very desirable effects were observed during the first year. The physicist Antonio bought a new pair of spectacles so he could once again read small print. Cardan the economist, who had been spending most of his time running a noodle factory, engaged an assistant professor (who could not challenge him for two years) to tutor him in the developments that had occurred in the field of economics during the previous fifteen years. The senior professor in chemistry announced in December, once he fully understood the plan, that for reasons of health he was retiring the next June, and several others followed him.

The library experienced an unprecedented rush. Learned journals—especially American—came out of dusty stacks, and hot disputes raged over the attempts of some men to draw out all of the modern treatises in a field. This, indeed, was the one clear disadvantage of the reform: men began to hoard knowledge. Few were willing to discuss their field except with better-informed people, and the exceptions were attributed to deceit as often as to arrogance. The graduate students suffered most: Filipo devoted his year course in the advanced theory of functions to a review of Euclid; Danto succeeded in getting many economics students to read Alfred instead of Adam Smith; and Ricard reviewed the Baconian theory, in painstaking detail, in his course on Shakespeare.

Yet the results of the competitions the following June were generally conceded to be beneficial. Several men began rapid, if overdue, movement toward retirement. Rumor had it that the unsuccessful and incompetent associate professor Jordan, whose wife was the daughter of the chairman of his department, was contemplating divorce. Pinzio became an associate professor.

Seguira in particular was delighted with the outcome. But he was worried by the tendency of teachers to devote their graduate courses to empty and irrelevant subjects; so he amended the regulations to grant five points (in a hundred) to a teacher for each of his students who won a challenge. This new rule led to careful calculation: would five points outweigh a superior performance by the student in the examination? The general belief was that professors gained, and assistant professors lost, by careful instruction. The scheme led to some paradoxes the following year: Dourni was challenged by seven of his graduate students and all got higher grades in the examination, but his thirty-five point bonus kept his position for him.

By the next autumn another unanticipated result of the reform became apparent. There was a precipitous fall in enrollments of graduate students, and it was soon discovered that all who could afford it had gone to the United States for graduate work. Seguira shared the professor's indignation at this maneuver, and vowed to amend the regulations the following spring. But meanwhile a heavy gloom settled on the staff: Were not the migratory students virtually studying the examination questions?

The gloom was justified by the fact. Of the sixty-one students who spent the year in the United States, forty-six won their challenge the following spring. Nor were the results so generally approved as the year before. It is true that several fossils continued thier steady march to the museum, and several able young men moved up another rank (Pinzio among them). But Storeo, the brilliant young astronomer, was defeated by a mediocre graduate student who—with the examiner—had spent the year studying some obscure variable stars. And Birnii fell because his magisterial command of political theory did not extend to the details of the New England township.

Seguira was in a quandary. To rule out migration was to invite charges of provincialism and inbreeding; to permit it on the current scale was to destroy graduate study.

He finally devised a compromise: the examinations
would be given by professors chosen at random from the
United States, England, France, Sweden, and Germany.
Now if a graduate student went abroad, four times out of
five he would guess the wrong country. The amendment
did stop the mass migration, but it had its own embar-
rassments: one sociologist had the same examination
question, by chance, in two consecutive years, and each
time gave the same answer. The first year he received an
ignominious flunk (from Stockholm), and the second
year he was offered a professorship (at Harvard).

And as the scheme entered its third year, a further effect could no longer be overlooked. Research had almost
stopped. Once observed, of course, it was easy to explain.
A man was likely to pass the examination with high
marks if he knew what others were doing; it did not help
his chances materially to do something himself. The faculty was becoming extremely well-read, and extremely
unenterprising. The most prominent exceptions showed
the advisability of the rule. Therespi had continued his
careful researches on the fruit fly and lost in two chal-
lenges. Laboro had finished the seventh volume of his
monumental history of South America, and flunked the
question on the Crusades.

Another year and some serious faculty losses were required to arouse Seguira to the importance of this problem. Once persuaded, he issued still another amendment:
a man was to receive two points for each article, and
seven for each book. He wanted to restrict these bonuses
only to current publications, but the opposition was too
strong. Even the younger men, especially the successful
younger men, were complaining of the baneful effects of

insecurity of tenure. And it was pointed out that definitive works required time—perhaps even two years. Seguira compromised by including all works published
within the previous decade.

The calculations of the faculty now became even more
complex. A book (seven points), or the training of a superior student (five points)? The writing of the book might
require three years, but the points were received every
year thereafter, whereas the student might eventually
leave. The answers at which the faculty finally arrived
were various. Cimoor, whose father owned a publishing
house, succeeded in getting out two books within the first
year, and so influential was his father that many of the
reviews were neutral. The political scientist Broze withdrew a book already in page proof, and published the
nineteen chapters as nineteen articles. This, however, oc-
casioned less complaint than Cardan's publication of a
book of readings. But still, research revived somewhat.

This sequence of felt difficulty and hopeful amendment, Pinzio said, might have gone on as long as the
unstable political foundations of Seguira's position permitted, had not two developments come to pass. The first
was the sudden dawning on Seguira that this patchwork
of rules was gradually obliterating the whole purpose of
his reforms. This was brought home during the next annual competition, when four professors came out of unwilling retirement and three, with the aid of their writings
of previous years, began again to climb the academic lad-
der. This particular development, of course, could be
dealt with through a new rule—but where was it leading?

The conjunction of the second event proved decisive.

Shortly after this awakening, Seguira received an invitation from the towering University of South America to become its rector. The regents wrote that his reputation for originality and enterprise was international, and that the success of his experiments indicated the need for a wider field of application. He accepted the new position, as much as a refuge as a promotion.

And what happened to Seguira? we demanded, and to the university? Seguira became as conservative as his reputation would allow, Pinzio assured us. And the merit system? Only one more amendment was added: a man could receive a permanent bonus of any number of points the department chairman deemed fit, when an offer was received from another university.

2

Specialism: A Dissenting Opinion

One subject on which almost all academic specialists agree is the evils of specialism. My university and many others impose courses in contemporary civilization or general science on the students to give them a well-rounded view of the universe. The view certainly will not have many edges when economics is taught by historians, and psychology is taught by economists. My university and many others contrive interdepartmental seminars to integrate the allied sciences and to explore some subject to its ultimate reaches. Some of these research teams have pushed so far that rescue parties will soon be necessary.

Specialism (like its cousin, the younger generation) would probably be mostly something to be deplored when one is in a nostalgic mood, were it not for the educational foundations. For the priests of these foundations, "the integration of knowledge" is the cry to perpetual battle with the sinning specialists. To them we owe (and

---

This is the only brave piece in the volume: defense of specialism in academic life ranks just above defense of racial prejudice.

are still paying for) some of the shiny ornaments of our intellectual life—the institute that "cuts across conventional lines" and the interdisciplinary project.

It is my thesis that this worship of the cosmopolitan mind is romantic foolishness. As a gesture toward consistency, I shall illustrate my arguments in support of this position from the field of economics rather than attempt to glean a variety of examples from other disciplines of which I lack a thorough (specialized) knowledge. Out of consideration for noneconomists, however, I shall take my illustrations from "general" economics rather than from my own field of specialization (homogeneous oligopoly).

The Division of Labor

One man working alone can make perhaps twenty pins in a day. If the task is divided among ten men, each of whom specializes in doing a part of the work, they can make 48,000 pins each day, or 4,800 pins per man. With this famous example, Adam Smith put the division of labor among the great organizing principles of social activity, and for two centuries or more men have prospered by pushing the principle into every nook of economic life and also into every nook of intellectual life. It is essential for the young scholar to specialize: only in this way can he acquire more knowledge than his older and more experienced colleagues. Indeed, for both the young and the old scholar there are only two defenses against the accumulation of knowledge: generalization and specialization, and of these the latter is more efficient.

For example, Wesley C. Mitchell specialized in the

study of business cycles and extended our knowledge much beyond that of his predecessors; now many specialists are studying the cycles in particular industries or economic processes, and are adding greatly to the knowledge Mitchell accumulated. Again, thirty years ago men began to estimate national income. The precision and detail of these estimates have increased continuously as men specialized in estimating particular components of the national income, such as incomes of independent professional men and incomes of financial institutions.

This is as trite as water: specialism is the royal road to efficiency in intellectual as in economic life. The widely trained individual simply cannot hold his own in any field with the individual of equal ability and energy who specializes in that field. Indeed, the individual who now attempts to survey a whole science or discipline is viewed as a popularizer ("journalist") or even as a charlatan, but definitely not as a creative scholar. It is notorious that when a man combines two diverse specialties, the members of each specialty acknowledge the man's eminence only in the specialty with which they are unfamiliar.

What Division Points?

Every specialist will admit the advantages of the division of labor. Since the modern specialist is equal in capacity to the less specialized scholar of former days, and only slightly more neurotic, it follows that the former knows more about that in which he specializes. *But*, it is said, many problems cross the boundaries that separate specialties, and they cannot be dealt with satisfactorily unless the specialist follows them, and this he is not able to do. In a more radical version, it is said that most problems of importance must be treated as wholes—the sum is more than the parts—and true understanding cannot be reached by any number of specialists.

Such remarks almost always rest on one or both of two propositions. First, that most real problems cross the boundaries of the specialties—in other words, the specialties are wrongly defined. Second, that all specialists of a given genre have the same knowledge and competence. Both of these propositions are wholly wrong.

The border "lines" of specialties are really zones, but let us ignore this for a moment. It should be obvious that the lines of division between specialties arose out of experience. No congress of academicians drew up the present lines of division. Instead, these lines of division developed pragmatically because they proved tenable and useful limits at which the investigation of considerable sets of important problems could be dropped without vitiating the results.

Economists, for example, rid themselves of psychology because they found that they could construct a body of theory that could deal with a wide set of important problems, and yield useful predictions, without building on a complicated theory of individual behavior. They rid themselves, at least for a time, of political science, because in the contemporary private-enterprise economy they were analyzing, the state played a relatively minor and unpervasive role.

Nor are these lines of division among specialists immutably fixed. They react to changes in the phenomena to be studied in the social sciences, and they react to changes in the state of knowledge in all sciences. Specialists are continually experimenting with new ranges of analysis to see if they can reach better understanding of their problems. It is a tribute to the significance of the current boundaries that most of these experiments are failures.

For example: each decade, for nine or ten decades, economists have read widely in the then-current psychological literature. These explorers have published their findings, and others in the field have found them wanting—wanting in useful hypotheses about economic behavior. Perhaps the next effort will be successful, and then economists shall quickly establish a new specialty, *psychonomics.*

Nor are the specialists a set of experts cast in one mold. No two of the creative minds in a discipline have the same knowledge, techniques, or interests. Some economic theorists are interested in the formal structure of the science, and work in fields like the theory of games and dynamic systems. Other theorists are interested in the substantive elements of the science, and work in fields like input-output analysis and the statistical analysis of demand. Some men are learned in mathematics; others can understand income tax returns; still others are students of the history of the discipline.

It is a gross impertinence for an outsider to tell specialists that they do not know how to deal with the problems in which they specialize. It is almost equally impertinent, and no more helpful, to assert that the problems which are dealt with by specialists are less important than other problems. Of course the "lines of division" between specialties may be inefficient at a given time, but only by employing successfully a new range of analysis will the inefficiency be demonstrated and located.

Teachers Are Different?

The hardy universalist may concede the greater efficiency of specialism and the fact that specialties are based upon reason, but he will nevertheless say that teaching is different. Specialism is good or at least a necessary evil in research, but in the classroom we need more widely trained individuals who can convey the essential unity of knowledge. I shall discuss this view only with respect to college education.

The good teacher is a mysterious person, and yet we must know his character before we can prescribe his training. In my view, the good teacher is not distinguished by the breadth of his knowledge, by the lucidity of his exposition, or by the immediate reactions of his students. His fundamental task is not to dispense information, for in this role he is incomparably inferior to the written word. His task is to fan the spark of genuine intellectual curiosity and to instill the conscience of a scholar—to communicate the enormous adventure and the knightly conduct in the quest for knowledge. (I realize that this view of the teacher's function will strike many as austere. They will emphasize the need for sympathetic development of the utmost in each individual, and turn teaching into coaching. I think they do a disservice to mediocre as well as to good minds.)

To this end, the fundamental requirements of the good teacher are competence (How can the incompetent be other than slovenly?) and intellectual vitality (How can the sedentary excite us to bold adventure?).

These traits may be acquired by wide reading and deep reflection, without engaging in research and becoming a specialist. But it is an improbable event. It is improbable psychologically: it asks a man to have the energy to read widely and the intellectual power to think freshly, and yet to do no research. He is to acquire knowledge and construct ideas—and keep them a secret. It is improbable scientifically: it asks a man to be competent in his under-standing of work that he has had no part in constructing. At least in economics, this is almost impossible. There is no book that states the consensus of the profession on the ideas that are changing—and these are naturally the most interesting ideas. Only the man who has tried to improve the ideas will know their strengths and weaknesses. Scholarship is not a spectator sport.

And so, according to my view of the good teacher, al-most invariably he will engage in research, and if this re-search is to be professionally respectable, it must be specialized research. Then his standards of intellectual performance are maintained by the critical scrutiny of his fellow scholars. The teacher who does not publish must have the conscience of a saint if he is not to take things easy: to pontificate instead of to reason; to conjecture rather than to know. It is not good for a man to associate only with his inferiors, and students are vastly the teacher's inferior in prestige and status.

When the search for universalism goes so far that men teach outside their general area of competence, the re-sults seem to me completely bad. The students are sub-jected to diffident reports on the reading of the teacher.

The teacher is compelled to spend a huge amount of time acquiring even the minimum knowledge necessary to last out the class hour. He tires of saying that he does not know the answers to reasonable questions, and acquires the habit of making up answers, and the students come to believe that a nodding acquaintance with many subjects is the earmark of the educated man.

The Last Stand

Even those who find the foregoing arguments convincing will refuse to welcome their message. Why do they cling to the goal of the universal mind?

Partly it is moon-reaching. It would indeed be fine to know many disciplines, I suppose, although heaven knows the ground shifts fast enough in debates even now. It would also be fine to have a salary of $100,000 a year.

Partly too, it is a humble confession of every man that he has failed to learn many things he would now cherish, and feels that with a broader training these painful gaps in his knowledge would be smaller and (what is more doubtful) that he would still know all he does now of his specialty. Yet such gaps in knowledge are inevitable so long as men are free to change their interests and work, to say nothing of deficiencies of elementary and secondary education.

And partly, too, it is a recognition of the sad fact that the most consummate mastery of a specialty may not prevent a man from playing the fool in other areas. We hope that the lessons of logic and evidence are universal in their applicability, but they seem to have a tendency to stick to their subject matter. At least, it is all too easy to name specialists whose logical ability and standards of evidence collapse when they step outside their specialties. But this is a defect of the man, not of his training and work. He lacks a general intelligence even if he has a partial genius. Specialism does not cause his deficiency; rather it tends to restrict him to the area where the deficiency is not present.

Are we, then, to become a race of guilds? Are we to converse easily and fruitfully with our fellow specialists but to be overcome by gauche silences in our association with other kinds of specialists? We can easily avoid this outcome. Let us all specialize a little in one field—it does not matter whether it is romantic music or interplanetary communication or the fruit fly or judicial review. Then we shall have a common meeting ground on which to have pleasant and profitable jousts of knowledge and wit, and on which we can form some estimate of the quality of a man. I leave to the specialists in social communication the selection of the precise field.

3

The National Commission as an Instrument of Controlled Impartiality

Of the dozens upon dozens of governmental and private commissions, the most recent (as of December 1960) to report was the Commission on National Goals. Let us consider its membership:

Henry M. Wriston, former president of Brown University (chairman)

Frank Pace, Jr., former secretary of the Army, now of General Dynamics Corporation

Erwin D. Canham, editor, Christian Science Monitor

James B. Conant, former president of Harvard University

Colgate W. Darden, Jr., former governor of Virginia, president of the University of Virginia

Crawford H. Greenewalt, president, Dupont

Of all the objectionable methods of persuasion, the use of false authority seems to me the most immoral—more so even than physical coercion.

Alfred M. Gruenther, president, American Red Cross

Clark Kerr, president, University of California

James R. Killian, Jr., chairman, M.I.T.

George Meany, president, AFL–CIO

It is at least a fair sample of the membership of national commissions: distinguished educators (possibly too many in this case), appropriately prominent businessmen and union officials, a representative or two of the huge nonprofit foundation industry, and a name or two from the fourth and other estates.

We might ask: Why did not each of these men write his own set of goals for America? And why did not each of the several members of the Randall Commission tell us how to conduct our foreign economic policy? Why does not each of the numerous members of the National Monetary Commission give us his own ideas on a good monetary system? And similarly for the thirty members of the Rockefeller Brothers Fund, which has touched upon every aspect of our life.

The question is childlike in its simplicity; I doubt that the answers would share this simplicity. It will in high probability be said that each man's personal statement would not have the breadth of vision, or rest upon the variety of knowledge, the diversity of viewpoint, that the group as a whole possesses. Quite true, no doubt. And yet what is the mysterious alchemy of committee proceedings that preserves each man's virtues, and weeds out each man's prejudices and blind spots?

There *is* such an alchemy in collaboration on technical matters: if a chemist and a lawyer collaborate on devising a chemical patent, the work is better than either could do because they have skills that supplement each other. But in the more conventional task of telling the nation what to do, there is no such expertise—almost everything basic is a question of judgment and of the values one places on high.

And in devising policy, the commission seeks to do precisely the opposite of adding the special knowledge possessed by each member: it seeks the largest common denominator of all of their prejudices and interests. A very extensive set of dissents will destroy any impact the report of the commission might have—the reader will instinctively feel that if the commission cannot convince itself of the wisdom of its views, no outsider should take the report very seriously. Only a moderate amount of skilled dissent is tolerable.

There is one other inevitable force that helps a committee to get out a report: no man feels that it must represent exactly his own viewpoint. If he were so individualistic (and possibly egotistic) as to believe so, then he would never accept membership on a commission, except to sabotage it—and one such performance would be enough to take him off the eligible list.

I have made a very strong statement: *that a commission's report does not and cannot reflect the strengths of its individual members.* Let me illustrate it.

The Commission on National Goals is not very fair game because its task was inherently impossible. One example will suffice to reveal its stance. The commission included several experts on labor unions—practitioners such as George Meany and Crawford Greenewalt as well as a distinguished academic specialist, Clark Kerr. This is the sum total of their (and the other seven's) wisdom on this troubled area:

Collective bargaining between representatives of workers and employers should continue as the nation's chief method for determining wages and working conditions.

Conferences among management, union leaders, and representatives of the public can contribute to mutual understanding of problems that affect the welfare of the economy as a whole.

Corporations and labor unions must limit the influence they exert on the private lives of their members. Unions must continue to develop adequate grievance procedures and greater opportunities for legitimate opposition.

These generalities do not have the merit of being goals (everything is machinery) or of being correct (collective bargaining is much less important than competition in fixing wages and working conditions).

The Rockefeller Brothers Fund somehow enticed twenty distinguished individuals—this time very heavily loaded with academicians, but chaired by Nelson Rockefeller—also to tell us where and how to go. Its report, *The Challenge to America: Its Economic and Social Aspects*, provides innumerable examples of commissionese. One could spend a long time on its specific recommendations, of which my favorite is: "The present double standard of regulation as between common carriers on the one hand and contract and private carriers on the other is basically unsound and a single standard of regulation should be developed where possible." This bold, nay, heroic, recommendation says we should extend or contract the regulation of motor trucking.

These examples could be multiplied, but not with profit. Committees are devices to keep individuals from going very wrong, not devices to reach truth where the policy issues are seriously controversial or the analytical or factual questions are complex. No commission has ever solved a hard problem in any intellectual sense; at its rare best, a commission has split or overawed the opposition.

Why, then, form commissions? And if they are formed, why not have each member state his own beliefs clearly and emphatically—letting the reader make for himself the synthesis that the committee's deliberations now seek to achieve?

The most important answer, I am convinced, is that the commission is deemed an efficient instrument of propaganda. The many semi-unanimous voices will somehow sound louder in chorus than the sum of their individual efforts.

The whole art of commissionmanship is to select honorable and disinterested members who will mostly agree with the position that the creators of the commission desire. This is not so difficult as it may sound, because most honorable and disinterested men of distinction (1) have no very definite ideas on most specific questions (in this they are no different from the rest of us), but (2) have definite, known sentiments and inclinations; and hence are predictable.

No one can create an impressive commission which will recommend that Castro be given Florida, but it would be easy to construct equally distinguished and impartial groups to recommend that future exploitation of atomic energy for peaceful uses be primarily public, or, if one wishes, primarily private. It would be just as easy to make up a fine commission to support, or oppose, an im-

mensely expanded federal urban renewal program, or increased (or decreased) foreign aid, or, in fact, either side
of any question that is really debatable in the near future.
A good chairman and a good knowledge of the men who
make up the slowly changing panel of eligible commission members are all that one needs.

Not all commissions are created primarily to propagandize particular policy views. Some are created only to
buy time: a commission will surely take at least six
months or a year to report, and meanwhile the passions
or crisis that called it into existence may have subsided.
And there are politicians and foundation heads—the only
two respectable sources of large funds for public commissions—who are so naive as to believe that the commission is an appropriate instrument for uncovering
truth, or confirming it. I suspect that this is the origin of
the Goals Commission, just as it was the origin of one
(the Attorney General's National Committee for the
Study of the Antitrust Laws—sixty-five members) of
which I was a member.

If the commissions are primarily propaganda instru-
ments, why do the distinguished citizens join them, attend the meetings, thumb the reams of staff papers, and
sign a document that most imperfectly represents their
individual views? Simply because they, too, are propa-
gandists. They will have signed a report that moderately
misrepresents their views on ten questions, but their
strongly held eleventh position got in, or at least part way
in. If they have no strong views, then they are simply
propagandizing themselves—joining the public-spirited,
enlightened leaders of the community, adding nice lines
to their *Who's Who* entries.

Academicians have another reason for joining: the desire to avoid displeasing the important persons—and, in particular, foundations—who push the commissions. The friendship of a foundation is second in importance only to a professor's professional reputation, and within considerable limits the friendship will be an adequate substitute for reputation.

I do not conclude that commissions would be excluded from the good society, and not only because this is so grave an issue that a commission should deal with it. Those commissions that buy time are often splendid social assets—they provide a cooling-off period for public passions, a function the United States Senate no longer fulfills so efficiently. Those that propagandize—that is, most of the other commissions—are finding that competition, the life of trade, can become the death of influence. Commission reports are now so numerous as to have become unimportant. Yet they will undoubtedly persist, unless displaced by some more dramatic innovation such as the summit conference, until a fateful day. That day, the theory of probability tells us, must eventually come: *two* distinguished and impartial commissions will simultaneously issue conflicting reports. Then the secret will be out: bringing twenty men together for eighty hours yields a weak formulation of somebody's ideas.

4

The Economics of Conflict of Interest

When Charles E. Wilson appeared before the Senate Committee on Armed Services, his confirmation as secretary of defense was eventually made contingent upon the sale of the 39,470 shares of General Motors stock he owned. The committee emphasized the importance of a secretary free of any commercial entanglements; Senator Lyndon Johnson's advice was unequivocal: "I think you should make the decision that you are going to divest yourself of any holdings that you might be called upon to make a decision in connection with."[1] The divestiture, the senator emphasized, should be complete: he implied dissatisfaction with placing the stock in a "trust, where ultimately it might come back to you."[2]

At the time of the confirmation hearings, the common

1. U.S. Senate, Committee on Armed Services, *Hearings*, January 23, 1953, p. 114.
2. Ibid, p. 109.

A complaint about one of the hypocrisies of American political life.

stock of General Motors amounted to some 88 million shares, so Wilson owned about one share in 2,200. An economist finds it difficult to believe that this stake would have influenced even a man who was much less honest than Wilson palpably was. Suppose that by dint of ceaseless and effective (and therefore also concealed) efforts, Wilson had managed to get an extra $1 billion of contracts beyond its fair share for General Motors during his period of office. On this then-great sum, the company would have earned about $70 million after taxes—at least, this was its rate of profit in 1952. Wilson's share as a stockholder would have been about $30,000, and at least $7,500 would have had to be subtracted from this for taxes if General Motors had paid out the usual share as dividends. What manner of millionaire would risk his reputation for $22,500?

In the ordinary ranges of stock ownership, the rewards from favoritism or worse are simply inadequate. The official runs all the risks of detection and obloquy but receives only one-thousandth or one-millionth of the proceeds. Even a narrow, grasping man will find this disproportion between risks and profits uninviting.

Of course, a man may own a large share of a company, so that of every $10 the company earns he gets $1 or $3 or $5. Andrew Mellon was in this position as a major stockholder in Aluminum Company of America and other companies, and in the eleventh year of Mellon's term as secretary of the treasury, Wright Patman sought his impeachment. We would not now admire the defense that Mellon did not personally own 50 percent of the stock of the companies, and, short of control, no question of conflict could arise—which was the defense then made.[3] I know of no reason even to hint that Mellon was influenced by his financial interests, and the odds are surely five thousand to one against the possibility of his using his position to profit to the extent of $55 million. That sum was the cost to him of the gallery he gave to the nation.

Yet the juxtaposition of large localized interests and great political power was uncomfortable. Subordinates might have done things Mellon would never have dreamed of doing, in a mistaken desire to please him. Or a man of shoddy character might feather another nest— and laws must be written to cover such men as well as gentlemen.

The extent of conflict of interest is quantitative, and quantitative questions do not admit of nice distinctions. A wealthy individual simply cannot put his wealth in such a form that our omnipotent state could not affect its value. Government bonds and dispersed urban real estate will be much less susceptible to manipulation than stock in a company that specializes in dealing with the Department of Defense. Tax benefits are immensely more valuable than government purchases because a tax dollar conferred is a dollar received, whereas a dollar of purchases conferred is—with luck—ten cents of profit (after costs) received.

The conflict of interest is at its maximum when the public official receives all of the payments for any benefit he confers. This situation is usually realized not in the

3. U.S. House of Representatives, Committee of the Judiciary, *Charges of Hon. Wright Patman against the Secretary of the Treasury*, 72d Cong., 1st Sess., H.R. 92 (1932), p. 71.

field of property, but in the field of labor services. The official who confers a vast boon upon a company can be paid in legal cash by being hired by the corporation at a suitable salary. The statutes on conflict of interest recognize this evident possibility by prohibiting the former public official from representing the company before the government in his area of public service for a period of two years; but this is no serious limitation upon the scope for compensation. I would conjecture that for every time a partial-minded official took his rewards in dividends, there have been twenty who joined a payroll.

The large number of resignations from public service for financial or "personal" reasons is hardly evidence of prior misdeeds. A public official who gains fame for the excellence of his work will also be able to retire to a more remunerative position without ever having deviated a millimeter from rectitude. Moreover, it is vastly easier for a mediocre man to achieve eminence by a tour of duty in Washington than by any other activity of comparable length, so Washington can in fact recruit men at relatively low salaries through this system of deferred compensation. I do not believe that more than an infinitesimal fraction of retirements from public service involves payments for special services performed. That infinitesimal fraction surely far exceeds the fraction consisting of those who gain by property income.

The delayed compensation for special services by way of preferred employment is essentially impossible to prevent or detect. The connection need seldom be overt and suspicious—in fact, with careful arrangements it probably need never be. The compensation for personal services has only one serious drawback: it depends upon living that long. The problem of conflict of interest is sometimes discussed with respect to the judiciary, although with our practice of lifetime tenure for judges it is surely of negligible significance here; there is no later period in which to reward the partial.

Conflicts of interest arise wherever one man is an agent for another; the agent does not bear the full consequences of his actions. The world of business has always faced the potential divergence of interests, and the activities of purchasing agents are a traditional area of concern. There is no evidence that conflicts of interest are more successfully resolved in the business world than they are in political life, but I conjecture that they are better handled in industry. There are rewards for the superior or subordinate who detects malfeasance in business, whereas the rewards for the detection of double dealing in political life go chiefly to the people out of power—precisely those who are least well situated to detect it.

5

Stigler's First Law of Sympathy

The Previous Literature

The heroic figure in the scientific analysis of sympathy, before the appearance of this essay, was Freud. Writing with incandescent intuition and a command of the literature that is fortunately uncommon, he addressed himself squarely to the central problem treated here: the construction of a law of sympathy that describes precisely the relationship between the quantity of sympathy and the object of the sympathy.

This problem became, indeed, a fixation: Freud recurred to it in a score of his lesser-known essays, seeking by an immensely resourceful panoply of methodologies to demonstrate the existence of such a law. We must attach the heaviest significance to his final, definitive, and

This paper received the Award of the Interdisciplinary Knot from the Center for Advanced Study in the Behavioral Sciences. Its characters have been thinly disguised for publication, except for my lamented friend Sidney Siegel. He would, I am sure, rather have one facet of a remarkable personality caricatured than be given flimsy anonymity.

lugubrious assessment of the prospects for finding such a law: "Es ist ganz unmöglich."[1]

The famous intradisciplinary research team known as Arroh-Friedmon-Reader-Soloh has recently renewed the attack upon this problem, employing the most powerful techniques of modern mathematical economics, including ridicule, only to reach the same conclusion as Sam Freud. Their results culminated in what they termed the AFRS Theorem: "If S is sympathy, and RS is any regularity in the behavior of S, then RS is topologically indifferent." But the team, as its last joint act, has since repudiated this theorem,[2] and now three much weaker propositions have been offered in its stead, each an individual effort:

Proposition A: If S is sympathy, then S belongs to A.

Proposition F: Scientific laws are provided at a minimum cost in optimum quantity by a well organized price system.

Proposition S: Sympathy is not a durable commodity.

Only Proposition F calls for brief, and cavalier, comment.

Friedmon offers (without price) three arguments in defense of the proposition that the offer of an adequate sum for a law of sympathy would have called forth such a law, if one existed. His first proof is that potato chips are supplied in this manner; this proof fails because potato chips

1. S. Freud, "Schrecklichkeit Noch Einmal," *Gesammelte Schriften,* vol. 14, p. 27.

2. One member, who prefers to remain anonymous, writes: "My . . . colleagues have slopped again, and I would appreciate if it you would refer not to the AFRS Theorem, but to the AFS Fallacy."

are different from sympathy. His second proof is that the Russians, who do not have a well organized price system, have no law of sympathy; this proof fails because he cannot read Russian. His final proof, if such it may be called, is that competition always works well, and scholars are competitive; but he forgets—although for him this must have been especially difficult—that not all scholars work.

The most recent work in this tradition has been done by the experimentalist Sidney Siegel, Ph.D.[3] Siegel produced suitable objects of sympathy under laboratory conditions and then measured the amount of sympathy they elicited. The objects of sympathy were a set of students who were subjected to tortures ranging from a hot foot to what the experimentalist describes as "scenes difficult to view with composure even before the next of kin arrived." As the measure of sympathy, each observer was asked to draw a coin from one of three buckets. These buckets contained, respectively, pennies, nickels, and twenty-dollar gold pieces, and the observer was asked to withdraw a coin proportional to the sympathy he felt for the student in the iron cage. Siegel found that sympathy is always at a maximum: whether the observer was laughing callously or sobbing in utter misery, he or she always withdrew a twenty-dollar gold piece, which under the conditions of the experiment he or she was entitled to keep.

Siegel's demonstration that sympathy is always at a maximum is structured, and therefore well worth the $13 million in twenty-dollar gold pieces his study cost the Ford Foundation. But this usually careful experimentalist

3. In *The Uses of Stanford Graduate Students.*

did not notice that his design contained one crucial flaw, which vitiates the results: the bucket with the twenty-dollar gold pieces had better illumination. One may also raise a question, or at least an eyebrow, at his collection of observers for the experiments: it is surely remarkable that under random sampling with replacement, the observers were: Henry Siegel (100 times), Horace Siegel (50 times), Hortense Siegel (700 times), and Mrs. Sidney Siegel (remainder of times).[4]

Genesis of My First Law

I customarily begin the day at a sedentary pace.[5] After an ice-cold shower lasting twenty minutes, I read one of the *New York Times*'s Hundred Neediest Cases to maintain a sense of well-being. I then eat a light breakfast and compose a stanza of my romantic epic, *Science Is a Boy's Best Friend*.

But things were very different on April 11, 1946. For one thing, I had not gotten to bed the previous night, and so did not have to arise. For another, I was in a railroad station. And for still another, I was feeling sorry for myself—a fugitive sentiment due to acute financial distress, a sick child, a threatening letter from my wife in Reno, and a grand jury indictment. And then it happened, a characteristic instance of serendipity. My sympathy for

4. in a recent letter from the French Riviera, Siegel's secretary writes: "M. Siegel now believes his table of random numbers contained misprints."

5. I describe the discovery of my first law only as a contribution to the sociology of science. Hasty readers may prefer to skip this section, and careful readers to go back to the first section. I am indebted to Kenneth Burke for writing between the lines.

myself, I carelessly calculated, was at the rate of 127 units per minute, and the vagrant thought flitted through my mind: How sorry was I for other people? I was about to dismiss the query with an offhand "enough," when it occurred to me that my sympathy for a person fell off, the more distant he was. And he could be far away not only in a geographic sense, but also socially. Would it not be possible to construct a vast social law corresponding to Newton's law for physical bodies, but naturally superior because distance was a more complex concept in social relations?

I kept putting this line of thought out of mind, but finally the handsome young lady on the bench facing me got her stocking straightened and I recurred to it. Its plausibility mounted, and I vowed to dedicate my time and talents to its development.

For several years I worked with a zeal, tenacity, and resourcefulness that modesty will not allow me to describe. And to no avail. The shrewdest hypothesis was contradicted by evidence; the most brilliant conjecture crashed upon the shoal of inconsistency. I grew sorrier for myself, and at one point my self-sympathy attained the rate of 197 units per minute.[6]

In the fall of 1950 the outlook was so bleak that I contemplated abandonment of the scholarly life for that of the concert violinist. A chance encounter with one Frank Reach did much to end this sterile period. We met in a Sausalito bar, and I eagerly poured my tale of woe into his receptive ear. His initially cheerful, not to say flushed,

6. I wish to express my debt to T.P. for performing on his abacus the tedious statistical calculations, and to John Thukey for challenging their accuracy.

countenance turned somber and finally despondent, and he suggested that we both consult a psychiatrist. He had heard of a Dr. Samage, unusual among his craft in possessing a two-person couch. I remember little of the session—the damp weather had forced Frank and me to take preventive ministrations against pneumonia—except that Dr. Samage's second question (his first concerned financial resources) was directed to Frank, and asked for a recounting of the occasions on which the subject of sex had entered his head. In all candor, Frank appeared to have a one-track mind.

The next day I was the subject of analysis, and, as I recall, the conversation went as follows:

Dr.: What's eating you, chum?

I: Misfortune is my mistress.

[*To be continued, perhaps, in a future year.*]

6

Festschriften

"Professor Ausgeschrieben," I said, "I promised to contribute an article to the Festschrift for Professor Geplänkel—he once got me an offer form Chicarvard and I felt I owed it to him. But time has slipped by, and here I am three weeks from the deadline without an idea."

Ausgeschrieben partially opened one eye, but the lid quickly fell back into place. "Giorgio," he replied, "it is simple. Have you a good article on hand? No? An article? No? A rejected article? No? Lucky. Then take one of the old ones—say, the one on what Pascal would have thought of indifference curves—and do it over with a few nice references to Geplänkel's *Eléments d'économie symétrique.*"

This sounded too simple, and a trifle jaded. So I drifted over to Ballpoint (fourteen Festschrift contributions).

I once undertook to review a Festschrift, which, as I recall, sought to honor a famous European economist. This is what came out, and was rejected by the Journal of Political Economy. *It is printed in its entirety.*

Ballpoint was, as usual, on the ball and to the point. "Take that idea you've been peddling at lunch—that only by eliminating marriage can we recruit a sufficient number of good elementary-school teachers—surround it with statistics, and send it in." This was good advice, and Ballpoint had used it ofen, but I simply cannot inflate a random idea into a purposive paper.

So I sought out Zweistein: "Geplänkel isn't a bad man, even considering that 1936 article on the artichoke cartel, and a Festschrift can be justified. The Festschrift honors him not only by its existence but also by the unfavorable comparison it makes with his work. So don't take this too seriously. Do the best that circumstances permit and remember that no one will buy the book."

I sat down and began to write: "The celebrated Pascal, it is true, never wrote on indifference curves. Yet if one interprets his work with the aid of Geplänkel's profound schemata, there emerges a picture . . ."

7

The Conference Handbook

There is an ancient joke about two traveling salesmen journeying together on a train. The younger drummer is being initiated by the elder into the social life of the traveler. They proceed to the smoking car, where a group of drummers have congregated. One says, "Eighty-seven," and a wave of laughter goes through the group. The older drummer explans to the younger that they travel together so often they've numbered their jokes. The younger drummer wishes to participate, and diffidently ventures to say, "Thirty-six." He is greeted by a cool silence. The older drummer takes him aside and explains that they've already heard that joke. (In another version, the younger drummer is informed that he has told the joke badly.)

This parable has often recurred to me on the occasions when I have attended conferences of economists. Econo-

I once refused classroom aids on the ground that I did not wish to let down the barriers to progress in a profession that had resisted all such progress for hundreds of years. Yet here I am doing exactly that!

mists travel together a great deal, and there is no reason why the discussions that follow the presentation of papers should not utilize a handbook of commentary. The following is a list of numbered comments—a list that, although preliminary, will cover a large share of the comments elicited in most conferences. If the proposal meets approval, the list can be extended, and a second list of the standard replies to these comments can be provided.

Introductory Remarks

A. The paper is a splendid review of the literature, but unfortunately it does not break new ground.

B. The paper admirably solves the problem that it sets for itself; unfortunately, this was the wrong problem.

C. What a pity that the vast erudition and industry of the author were misdirected.

D. I am an amateur in this field, so my remarks must be diffident and tentative. However, even a novice must find much to quarrel with in this piece.

E. I can be very sympathetic with the author; until two years ago I was thinking along similar lines.

F. It is good to have a nonspecialist looking at our problem. There is always a chance of a fresh viewpoint, although usually, as in this case, the advantages of the division of labor are reaffirmed.

G. This paper contains much that is new and much that is good.

H. Although the paper was promised three weeks ago, I received it as I entered this room.

Comments

1. Adam Smith said that.
2. Unfortunately, there is an identification problem that is not dealt with adequately in the paper.
3. The residuals are clearly nonnormal and the specification of the model is incorrect.
4. Theorizing is not fruitful at this stage: we need a series of case studies.
5. Case studies are a clue, but no real progress can be made until a model of the process is constructed.
6. The second-best consideration would, of course, vitiate the argument.
7. That is an index number problem (obs., except in Cambridge).
8. Have you tried two-stage least squares?
9. The conclusions change if you introduce uncertainty.
10. You didn't use probit analysis?
11. I proved the main results in a paper published years ago.
12. The analysis is marred by a failure to distinguish transitory and permanent components.
13. The market cannot, of course, deal satisfactorily with that externality.
14. But what if transaction costs are not zero?
15. That follows from the Coase theorem.
16. Of course, if you allow for the investment in human capital, the entire picture changes.
17. Of course, the demand function is quite inelastic.
18. Of course, the supply function is highly inelastic.
19. The author uses a sledgehammer to crack a peanut.

20. What empirical finding would contradict your theory?

21. The central argument is not only a tautology, it is false.

22. What happens when you extend the analysis to the later (or earlier) period?

23. The motivation of the agents in this theory is so narrowly egotistic that it cannot possibly explain the behavior of real people.

24. The flabby economic actor in this impressionistic model should be replaced by the utility-maximizing individual.

25. Did you have any trouble in inverting the singular matrix?

26. It was unfortunate that the wrong choice was made between M_1 and M_2.

27. That is all right in theory, but it doesn't work out in practice (use sparingly).

28. The speaker apparently believes that there is still one free lunch.

29. The problem cannot be dealt with by partial equilibrium methods: it requires a general equilibrium formulation.

30. The paper is rigidly confined by the paradigm of neoclassical economics, so large parts of urgent reality are outside its comprehension.

31. The conclusion rests on the assumption of fixed tastes, but of course tastes have surely changed.

32. The trouble with the present situation is that the property rights have not been fully assigned.

8

A Sketch of the History of Truth in Teaching

The future is obscure, even to men of strong vision, and one would perhaps be wiser not to shoot arrows into it. For the arrows will surely hit targets that were never intended. Witness the arrow of consumerism.

It started simply enough: various people—and especially a young man named Nader—found automobiles less safe than they wished, and quite possibly than you would have wished. They demanded and in a measure obtained, if not safer cars, at least cars that were ostensibly safer. A considerable and expensive paraphernalia of devices became obligatory in new cars. These zealous patrons of the public furthermore insisted that defective products be corrected, and that damage arising in spite of the most conscientious efforts of the manufacturer should be his financial responsibility. Similar arrows were soon launched at a score of nonvehicular industries.

I could testify to the historical accuracy of this account if I took the title less seriously.

This quiver of truth- and safety-minded arrows was thrown for a time at perfectly appropriate targets—businessmen accustomed to public abuse, who were naturally able to charge their customers for any amount of safety, frequent and successful lawsuits, and obloquy. But the arrows of reform pass through—if they hit at all—the targets at which they are aimed, and in 1973 they hit a professor. Evil day!

In that year a young man named Dascomb Henderson, a graduate of Harvard Business School (1969) and recently discharged as assistant treasurer of a respectable-sized corporation, sued his alma mater for imparting instruction since demonstrated to be false. This instruction—I will omit here its explicit and complex algebraic formulation—concerned the proper investment of working capital. One of Henderson's teachers at Harvard, a Professor Plessek, had thoroughly sold his students on a sure-fire method of predicting short-term interest rate movements, based upon a predictive equation incorporating recent movements of the difference between high- and low-quality bond prices, the stock of money (Plessek had a Chicago Ph.D.), the number of "everything is under control" speeches given by governors of the Federal Reserve Board in the previous quarter, and the full-employment deficit. It was established in the trial that the equation had worked tolerably well for the period 1960–1968 (and Henderson was exposed to this evidence in Plessek's course in the spring of 1969), but the data for 1969 and 1970, once analyzed, made it abundantly clear that the equation was capable of grotesquely erroneous predictions. Assistant treasurer Henderson, unaware of these later results, played the long-term bond market with his corporation's cash, and in the process the cash lost its surplus character. He was promptly discharged, learned of the decline of the Plessek model, and sued.

This was a new area of litigation, and Henderson's attorney deliberately pursued several lines of attack, in the hope that at least one would find favor with the court:

1. Professor Plessek had not submitted his theory to sufficient empirical tests. Had he tried it for the decade of the 1950s, he would have had less confidence in it.
2. Professor Plessek did not display proper scientific caution. Henderson's class notes recorded the sentence: "I'll stake my reputation as an econometrician that this model will not [engage in intercourse with] a portfolio manager." This was corroborated, with a different verb, by a classmate's notes.
3. Professor Plessek should have notified his former students once the disastrous performance of his theory in 1969 and 1970 became known.
4. Harvard University was grossly negligent in retaining (and hence certifying the professional competence of) an assistant professor whose work had received humiliating professional criticism (*Journal of Business,* April 1972). Instead, he had been promoted to associate professor in 1972.

The damages asked were $500,000 for impairment of earning power and $200,000 for humiliation.

Harvard and Professor Plessek asked for dismissal of the suit, claiming that it was frivolous and unfounded. Universities and teachers could not be held responsible for honest errors, or all instruction would be brought to a stop. Universities and professors could not be asked to disseminate new knowledge to previous students—this would be intolerably costly. In the lower court these defenses prevailed, and Judge MacIntosh (Harvard, LL.B. 1938) asserted that university instruction and publication were preserved from such attacks by the First Amendment, the principle of academic freedom, an absence of precedent for such a complaint, and the established unreliability of academic lectures. On appeal, however, Judge Howlson (Yale, LL.B. 1940) remanded the case for trial on the merits, and in the course of reversing Judge MacIntosh's decision, remarked: "It seems paradoxical beyond endurance to rule that a manufacturer of shampoos may not endanger a student's scalp but that a premier educational institution is free to stuff his skull with nonsense."

As the reader will know, Harvard and Professor Plessek won the case on the merits, but by a thin and foreboding margin. Only the facts that (1) the Plessek equation, as of 1969, looked about as good as most such equations, and (2) the plaintiff could not reasonably be expected to be informed of the failure of the equation as soon as two years after it was discovered—the lag in publication alone is this long—excused the errant professor. As for Harvard, it would have shared responsibility for the undisputed damage to the plaintiff if Plessek had been of slightly lower quality. So held the court of last resort, in a decision that professors read as carefully as a hostile book review.

The university world received the decision with what an elderly Englishman would call concern and I would call pandemonium. Professional schools—medicine as well as business—were quick to realize its implications. Within a breathless three weeks, a professor at Cornell's medical school had sent an explicit retraction of his treatment of Parkinson's disease to the last decade's graduates of the school. This proved to be only the first of a torrent of such actions; but well before that torrent had climaxed, at least ninety-five suits against universities and teachers had been filed. Along with the "recalls," as the retractions were called in honor of their automobile antecedents, the learned journals were flooded with statements of "errata" and confessions of error. A fair number of academic reputations fell suddenly and drastically.

The subsequent, explosively rapid expansion of litigation directed at error in teaching is not for this nonlegal writer to report. Many years and cases were required before a reasonably predictable set of rights and responsibilities could be established, and a man may find much to be angry about in these cases, whatever his position. That the lazy or stupid student was entitled to an exhaustive explanation for his failure in a course (*Anderson* v. *Regents,* 191 Cal. 426) was an intolerably expensive aberration—especially when the teacher was required to present a tape recording of the explanation. That a professor could not be held responsible for error in a field where truth and error frequently exchanged identities (*Neal* v. *Department of Sociology,* 419 Mich. 3), on the other hand, inevitably raised a challenge to the field to justify its existence. Rather than pursue either the main line of decisions or the aberrations, it seems preferable to look at the eventual effects of truth in teaching upon the universities. A conscientious observer must be cautious in his interpretation of the effect—even though the present essay is clearly exempt from challenge (*President Bowen* v. *Assistant Professor Holland*, 329 N.J. 1121, a tenure case)—so the following remarks are best viewed as plausible hypotheses.

In general, the new responsibility rested heavily upon those most able to bear it: those fields in which classification of given material as true or excusably false versus inexcusably false was easiest to establish with near unanimity. Theological schools were virtually exempted, and, oddly enough, also computer science. Mathematics was exempted because one could always look up the answer, and political science because one couldn't. The branch of economics dealing with how to enrich a new nation ("economic development" was the title) was actually forbidden by the courts, on the ground that no university could pay for the damage its teachers did.

In those subjects where truth in teaching bore most heavily—those where incorrect knowledge was costly and demonstrable, as medicine, chemistry, and tax law—the classroom became a very different place. Students were *forbidden* by most universities to take notes, which were instead supplied by the teacher, and the sneaky device of a tape recorder with hidden microphone was combatted vigorously, if not always successfully. Harvard's defense proved to have content: teachers were unwilling to introduce new ideas, but it can be argued that the net balance was favorable—much ancient nonsense also vanished, and courses often were completed in two weeks.

The learned journals underwent a remarkable transformation. Let me quote the introductory paragraph of an article on the nature of short-run price fluctuations in commodity prices (*Review of Economics and Statistics,* August 1978):

> The present essay presents a theory, with corroborating though inadequate evidence, that there is a set of nonrandom short-run movements in the price of "wheat." (The actual commodity analyzed is secret but will be revealed to professors on written waiver of responsibility.) The present essay is concerned only with methodology. Only the crudest beginning has been made, and it would be irresponsibly rash to venture money on the hypothesis. Also, the hypothesis is virtually identical with Reslet's (1967); I contribute chiefly a more powerful statistical technique (due to S. Stigler 1973), which has its own limitations. The regressions have been calculated three times, on different computers, with similar results.[1] The author will welcome, but not be surprised at, valid criticisms of the paper.

The superscript 1 referred to a footnote inserted by the editor of the *Review:* "The Board of Overseers of Harvard University expresses concern at the measure of nonrandomness in the residuals, which, if the author were a Harvard professor, would require a full departmental review of the manuscript." No wonder one scholar complained that there was more warning against reading his article than against smoking marijuana cigarettes!

The longer-term effects of truth in teaching are another story, which I shall not seek even to summarize here. The historic step was the creation in 1981 of the Federal Bureau of Academic Reading, Writing, and Research (BARWR). This body soon established licenses for participation in scholarly activities, and the license became a prima facie defense against the charge of incompetence. No university that employed an unlicensed teacher could receive federal grants, which by 1985 averaged 99.7 percent of university revenue.

The BARWR has instituted rigorous standards for the conduct of learned journals and is now inquiring into the possibility of establishing subject matters (for example, communistic theory) that are prima facie evidence of incompetence.

9

Meager Means and Noble Ends

I propose here to look at higher education through the morbid eyes of an economist. The economic side of education is not the most interesting side, even to an economist; but it is sufficiently important to invite at least a modest survey.

Higher education is a competitive industry—a large, reasonably prosperous competitive industry. Competitive industries display characteristic forms of behavior, which I hope my fellow economists will allow me to simplify into a set of rules. Though most of these rules are not essential to reach the conclusions about the future of this university at which I am aiming, let me state several and indicate their applicability to higher education, if only to persuade you that we are in fact in a competitive industry.

First, it is a well-known rule that an increase in the de-

This speech, delivered before the trustees of the University of Chicago, reveals secrets on how to create a great university. It does not, however, reveal the secret of how to get people really to want one.

mand for the product of a large competitive industry will produce a rise in its price unless the industry's technology is improving apace. I think it is fair to say that the technology of college teaching is not among the most dynamic branches of modern life. The last really notable advance in college teaching in recent times was the invention of the printing press. I find it suggestive of the pleasant stability of our teaching ways that the fact that books are now sold without bindings has been hailed as a major advance. Meanwhile the growth in the number of students has been immense, and—to use Chicago as an example—tuition, which is our price, has risen from $120 in 1895 to approximately $9,000 in 1984, an average of about 5 percent a year.

Second, if an industry's demand is growing rapidly, new firms will enter the industry on a large scale. Here again our colleges and universities fit the rule; in 1760 there were six colleges, or one for every 300,000 of population; in 1980 there were 2,000 odd colleges and universities, or one for every 116,000 of population. I have excluded normal schools and junior colleges from this count of schools, or the ratio would be one for every 70,-000 of population. Enrollments have risen faster than the number of schools, of course, so we have been moving away from, not toward, that professor sitting on a short log and talking to one student. I am reminded of a remark once made by a colleague at Brown University: after thirty years of teaching, he had concluded that it would be just as effective to sit on the student and talk to the log.

There are many more of these rules for competitive industries. One rule says that large industries will solicit a variety of favors from the state—tariffs, subsidies, preferential tax status, and what not. Our colleges excel in this activity: I believe that higher education is the only industry whose customers are housed at the expense of the federal government, and the only industry whose employees are provided with frequent, extended vacations abroad. Then there is the rule that as the individual enterprise grows, it uses more and heavier machinery, but let us not tax our overtaxed deans and vice-presidents. There is the rule that employees with seniority will seek to devise working rules that reduce to a tolerable level the strains of a rigorous occupation; in our industry this is described as getting time off for research.

I hope I have persuaded you that there is at least a family resemblance between higher education and other competitive industries. There are many differences between our industry, which produces knowledge, and those that produce commodities—and not all are favorable to the education industry. But I ask you only to accept the conclusion that the main forces of competition exert powerful and similar influences on all competitive industries. I wish to invoke now the rule in competitive industries which provides the theme of my remarks.

This rule is, in the words of the discoverer, that the division of labor is limited by the extent of the market. If Adam Smith were alive today, he would no doubt be here, for his scientific genius would have overshadowed, for the Department of Economics, his regrettably conservative tendencies. I would assure him that his rule has been one of great power and fertility in economic theory. Although the rule has wider scope, for our purposes it is a sufficiently extended interpretation to state that the specialization of industries, of the plants within industries, and of the laborers within plants all increase as an industry grows.

That there has been a continuous increase in the specialization of college teachers and researchers is a notorious fact, which I can illustrate within my craft. Adam Smith was appointed professor of logic at the University of Glasgow in 1751. Delayed by commitments at Edinburgh, he was substituted for by the professor of jurisprudence. On arriving in Glasgow, he in turn substituted for the ailing professor of moral philosophy, whom he soon succeeded, and taught jurisprudence, politics, rhetoric, and belles lettres. His lectures embraced natural theology, ethics, the history of civil society, tastes, and the history of philosophy, as well as containing some allusions to political economy. Today a professor of economics who pretended to be an expert in such far-flung fields as international trade and retail trade, or economic history and the history of economics, would be branded a charlatan. All this is trite, and I shall not pursue it beyond remarking that in a group this large there may even be two or three people who share my belief that this increase in specialization is desirable as well as inevitable.

When specialization is suggested for institutions of higher education, however, one flies in the face of the announced goal of every respectable college and university. Every school, be it major, minor, or diminished seventh, desires to be strong in *every* significant scholarly discipline—certainly in the traditional arts and sciences. The specialized institutions themselves are ashamed of their lack in this area, and the institutes for technical disciplines, such as M.I.T., boast of their growing strength in the social sciences and humanities. The university world says, with a singularly unanimous voice: let Cornell have hotel management, even let Washington have early Chinese literature; but Chicago, and Harvard, and Columbia, and Berkeley, and North-by-Northeast Methodist *must* be of the first rank in each of the basic sciences and humanities.

Rules are rules, and wishes are wishes. The wish of universal excellence is impossible to achieve. We cannot build plane triangles whose angles sum to 190 degrees, or universities that are uniformly excellent. Rather than treat this conclusion as a corollary, which would save me some trouble and you some time, I shall seek to establish it directly on the basis of two empirical propositions.

The first proposition is that there are at most fourteen really first-class men in any field, and more commonly there are about six. Where, you ask, did I get these numbers? I consider your question irrelevant, but I shall pause to notice the related question: Is the proposition true? And here I ask you to do some homework: gather with your colleagues and make up a numbered list of the twenty-five best men in one of your fields—and remember that these fields are specialized. Would your department be first-class if it began its staffing in each field with the twenty-fifth, or even the fifteenth, name? You have in fact done this work on appointment committees. I remember no cases of an embarrassment of riches, and I remember many where finding five names involved a shift to "promising young men," not all of whom keep their promises. I leave it to the professors of moral philosophy and of genetics to tell us whether the paucity of first-class men is a sort of scientific myopia, a love of invidious ranking, or a harsh outcome of improvident marriages. But the proposition is true.

My second proposition is that no one school has much in the way of financial resources. Let us measure the wealth of a school by the amount it spends on faculty salaries—this payroll is its effective demand for professors. Like all simple numbers this wages-fund is not an ideal measure, because a school's payroll would probably change in interesting ways if it decided to hire fewer and better men, but it is a sufficiently appropriate measure of buying power in the market for talented men. Then it is approximately true that the University of Chicago, with an academic wages-fund of $125 million in 1980, had about one-half of 1 percent of the total wages-fund of American universities and colleges, and perhaps 2 or 2.5 pecent of the wages-fund of the fifty largest universities. The richest of these fifty schools was probably Berkeley, with a wages-fund of $188 million, or perhaps 3.5 percent of the total of the elite; Harvard had about $182 million; Yale, $145 million.

No school, not even the richest, has a wages-fund sufficient to hire one of the six best men in each field within the traditional arts and sciences. Fifty or a hundred institutions seriously seek such men, and even the fiftieth in wealth—which is about one-fourth as rich as the first in wealth—can bid enough for one or two such leaders to make them prohibitively expensive to others. The richest museum cannot acquire all the Rembrandts, and the richest school cannot hire all the leaders.

The basic trends of our time are strengthening the forces of diffusion of able men among institutions. The state has taxed away great private fortunes and generously supported public institutions. I have no doubt whatever that those who administer direct governmental subsidies to education will develop quota systems calculated to ensure that each area and institution gets its share of the subsidies. The universally premier institution is becoming increasingly more unattainable. And the rules of economics make no exception for Chicago.

Economics is sometimes called the dismal science. I resent the phrase, for only young children should get angry at a corpus of knowledge that prevents hopeless and costly endeavors. To recognize a problem is to be better armed for rational actions, and I will now turn briefly to the actions I believe rational with the growth of specialization.

Universities will make their peace with the forces of specialization by making a choice that falls somewhere between two poles: a universal mediocrity, at one end; a select and none too lengthy list of truly distinguished departments, at the other. I diffidently interpret the tradition of Chicago to be that which I, too, desire: the preservation of preeminence in a dozen of the most durable and basic disciplines, with at least respectable competence in the remainder of the basic disciplines—and nothing more.

I need not argue for such a preference here, because quite frankly none of you has the courage to oppose it. No one, indeed, seems to have the courage to defend mediocrity in any human activity; we are all hopeless romantics in the face of the naked fact that mediocrity is a fairly high estate—beyond the reach of a third of

America's colleges and universities. Some people might quarrel with the limitation of my hopes, and tell me that in their field there are 1,400 leaders, one for each college and university. Some people might say that all Chicago has to do—a phrase which in this context means that all Chancellor of the Exchequer George Beadle has to do—is increase our endowment to, say, $10 billion next year. But I refuse to attribute these absurd views to a single one of you; the most meager compliment I can pay you is to assume that you accept the goal of selective eminence in light of the facts of competition.

Here I must pause to notice an objection, not to the goal of selective eminence, but to the view that it can consist of a scattering of distinguished departments throughout the university. It will be argued strongly by some men that this view of scattered excellence does not give due weight to the importance of cooperation between related fields—what the economist with his customary felicity calls complementarity. They will say that it is idle to speak of the possibility of outstanding departments of, say, physics and geophysics if chemistry and mathematics are weak; that an outstanding economics department requires outstanding history, political science, sociology, and statistics departments; and so on.

If this position is correct—if one department of a division can be eminent only on the condition that the other departments also are—then a very radical implication must be drawn. For this emphasis on complementarity does nothing to increase either the number of leaders in each field or the resources of a university. The implication must then be, quite simply, that selective eminence is still essential but must be achieved by making one division of the university—be it humanities, physical sciences, biological sciences, social sciences, or what not—and only this one division eminent, letting the remainder drift into respectable obscurity and possibly eventual oblivion.

I myself am skeptical that the complementarity of disciplines is this intimate and pervasive. There is no historical support for the view that the strength and achievements of any one social science depend intimately on the quality of the related social scientists—indeed I know of no evidence for this view even when one enlarges his vision from a single institution to the world of scholarship. Economics, for example, has had two golden ages in the last century, from 1870 to 1900, and from 1935 to 1950, in the latter case with time out for a war. None of the other social sciences contributed importantly to either of these periods of sustained creativity. It will take heavy argument to convince me that the situation is radically different in the other divisions.

Mind you, no one will argue that able colleagues in other disciplines are not of value. Of course they are valuable to the specialist. Even it they were not available, it certainly would be impossible to get along without their books—but I shall not digress to examine the disquieting thought that perhaps it is the library that is keeping us together. What I do say, and earnestly believe, is that the dependence between disciplines is not so intimate that it must be maintained day by day within a single quadrangle. Until this is shown to be generally the case, I shall continue to believe that it is possible for an eminent university, and not just an eminent division, to exist.

One does not implement the goal of selective eminence

for a university by telling some departments that they have been chosen for eminence and others that they have been condemned to respectability. There is room for chance, and the identity of the eminent departments will change slowly over time. There is more room for bold and gifted leadership, and it is a major attainable achievement to add two more to our preeminent departments.

But the goal of selective eminence cannot be pursued effectively if one ignores its selectivity. The goal cannot be achieved if we fail to be ruthless with proposals to increase our comprehensiveness: it is a fact of life that a vote for a school of journalism or an institute of automation is a vote to get rid of one or two first-class men in physics or anthropology or law. The goal cannot be achieved if we insist that every department be *almost* preeminent: a vote to hire two expensive number-twenty men is a vote to be rid of a number-one man. These are different ways of saying that we must steer the difficult course between easy achievement and romantic impossibility. Some women are not fastidious, and others insist upon marrying only perfect men. I know Chicago will not become a harlot; I do not want it to become a spinster.

I would add a word concerning a very troublesome lot who insist upon intruding into the discussions of their betters—I refer to the students. The student cannot achieve the best possible instruction in every specialized field at any one institution; this I shall now treat as a corollary. Though a student does not study every specialized field even within one department, he would often profit by dividing his time between institutions whose strengths complement one another. There would be much merit in the development, at the graduate level, of the practice of spending a half year or a year at a second institution. This practice, you will recall, was prevalent during the fourteenth century; and, on balance, transportation has improved since then (aside from parking). The student would also gain perspective by living for a time in a different intellectual atmosphere, and the professors—for whom things must be good if they are to be good for the country—would also gain by the diversity of students.

The competitive industry is not one for lazy or confused or inefficient men: they will watch their customers vanish, their best employees migrate, their assets dissipate. It is a splendid place for men of force: it rewards both hard work and genius, and it rewards on a fine, generous scale. The success of a competitive enterprise is not in the least uncertain if its employees are able and diligent and its leadership sane and courageous. No such guarantees of success are present for a monopolist: he is overwhelmingly dominated by forces over which he has negligible control. This paradox—that power deprives one of the certainty of success—is partly verbal, as all good paradoxes are, but it contains an important truth.

I rejoice, therefore, not as an economist but as an employee of a singularly successful young competitive firm, in our troubles. If money came only to those who already had it, we should never have existed. If great schools could easily get and retain all the able men, Chicago would never have been worth mentioning. If we dwelled in a pastoral college village, where neither squalor nor crime had ever been observed, it is likely also that intellectual ferment and adventure would be absent. I shall not allow rhetoric to carry me to the absurdity of saying that only severe hardship allows of progress. I do say that if we wish, we can become the most successful firm in the industry, in fifteen major product lines.

10

Freedom in the Academy

In the last twenty years the freedom to express unpopular ideas—unpopular, that is, with audiences—at American colleges and universities appears to have shrunk drastically. Certainly there have been more than enough shameful episodes of censorship.

If one searched hard enough, one could always find in our past too many examples of the harsh treatment of a teacher with "dangerous" tendencies or the grossly discourteous reception on campus of a maverick. In the late sixties, one would not have to search: Harvard University alone has provided enough shame for a dozen universities, and the only reason for singling it out by name is its premier status. The violence has receded in recent years, and the publicized acts of censorship have become infrequent. But this quiescence does not imply a growth

---

When this commencement talk was given at Carnegie-Mellon University, one faculty member was stimulated to hand out rejoinders within fifteen minutes of its completion. I hope you will study it with at least equal care.

of tolerance. Rather, provocation has diminished, as unpopular people have been left uninvited. When last did
a former secretary of state fail to receive a single invitation to lecture at a major university? What major university would have felt it safe, when bombing of North-
ern Vietnam resumed in December 1972, to offer a forum
to secretaries Laird or Rogers? Popular interest has declined in certain controversial subjects, but a decrease in
interest is not an increase in tolerance. The limits of
comfortable public discussion at our universities are con-
fining.

As an ardent supporter of unrestricted intellectual inquiry, I might naturally be expected to implore you, most
of whom are about to leave academic life (and high time,
too), to battle for academic freedom in the great world
outside. That would be an eminently sensible example of
what the economist calls the division of labor: the faculty
picks the battle, and the alumni are asked to fight it. I suspect that I would not be above such self-serving conduct,
but the assignment would be futile: the battle for academic freedom is being lost not outside the university,
but within.

Next, it would seem just as natural to harangue my fellow faculty, aided and abetted by the university administration, to combat the tyranny imposed upon professors
by obstreperous students. Certainly students and campus
hangers-on have often been the moving agent in the forc-
ible suppression of academic freedom in universities.
That would also be an easy theme: there are relatively
few future students here, and the rest of us could glow
with righteous virtue warmed by memories of Mario
Savio and Mark Rudd.

Again the solution will not do: the students have played only an instructed role in the decline of intellectual freedom in the university. In fact, I propose the hypothesis, which many or all of you will find wholly unbelievable, that students and the young generally behave in the manner in which we expect them to behave. Note that I did not say that they behave as we *tell* them to behave, but as we, by our own behavior, *teach* them to behave. The young are shockingly insecure, and they would not dare to launch an attack upon any institution in which the vast majority of the rest of us fervently believe.

It is painfully obvious who is left to be blamed for the decline of academic freedom: the faculty. What an absurd culprit! How could anyone believe that it is the professors who are suppressing freedom? Why, to be quite selfish and narrow of vision, should they take away some of their own prerogatives and protections? Whether for private or public purposes, did professors not fight the first Senator McCarthy and his ilk with intensity and perseverance?

Pretty questions, but easily enough answered in a moment. The fact is that academic freedom in its true meaning—the freedom to say unpopular things—is in its present low estate because professors do not use it. The students naturally rebel at a warlike cabinet officer—after all, when did they last hear an outspoken hawk among their admired professors? The students naturally shout down an Arthur Jensen or Richard Herrnstein—after all, for a long time no respectable sociologist or psychologist or educationalist would say anything that hinted at differences among races.

If American university faculties were indeed open to strongly divergent viewpoints, the students would hardly bother to harass a visiting lecturer for saying things similar to what they would constantly be hearing from their own faculty. But no: they have learned from the pronouncements of their faculties that certain views are beyond the pale. The united presidents of the Ivy League universities—speaking as private individuals, mind you —gave careful reassurance, on the heels of the Cambodian raid, that no decent human being could defend the war in Vietnam. Why then, indeed, should students tolerate a barbarian who is associated with that evil war? Similarly, harsh things may obviously be, and have been, said about professors from Rhodesia, professors who defend pollution, and other purveyors of "inexcusable" beliefs.

This assignment of blame for the novelty and hence unacceptability of unpopular views on campuses implies that somehow these views have been kept off campus, or at least locked inside the professors who hold them. The easy answer, surely the answer that leaps to most professorial lips, must be that naturally all professors are basically decent and intelligent, and therefore they shun inexcusable views. All wars are dreadful, and the Vietnam War was particularly immoral, so only indecent or ignorant or callous people would support it. Again, what intelligent individual could possibly defend anti-Semitism and racist views?

It would be pleasant to believe that the views which have been most forcibly excluded from expression in American universities are indubitably mistaken. No respectable university will promote an assistant professor of mathematics who sums a divergent infinite series, so why should it allow him to propose comparable errors in political or intellectual life? Unfortunately, this easy answer is pernicious arrogance: there are no certainties in science or in politics, in economics or in morals. Tautologies aside, we have abundant historical evidence that the ruling views of one period are the exploded fallacies, or at least the unperceptive superficialities, of a later time. If someone really believes that the verdict on the Vietnam War is as certain as a mathematical theorem, then *he* is sadly ignorant of history, including the history of mathematics.

No, the easy answer will not do: unpopular views have largely vanished from American campuses—not that their proponents were ever very numerous or outspoken—because there are strong sanctions against the hiring and promotion of holders of unpopular views.

The homogeneity of views (at least, of publicly expressed views) of American professors is remarkable. An occupation staffed with clever men, instructed to study the old and the new, and certainly the unfamiliar, has a narrower range of views than do physicians or lawyers. It is apparently impossible from published sources to measure this homogeneity of professorial views, but it is hinted at by the results of various polls; in 1972, for example, faculty at major universities cast about 10 percent of their votes for the successful candidate for U.S. president.

This homogeneity of view, this conformity to a given set of educated liberal standards, inheres in the very method by which professors are selected. At all respectable universities and colleges, the faculty is the primary power in the choice of new faculty and in decisions to promote or send away present faculty. The system has important strengths, but clearly it reproduces the procedures of a private club. Decisions are made by committee, and they are not made by simple majority vote: a conscious attempt is made to achieve consensus. A few strong opponents are sufficient to stop an appointment: a modified black ball is still in force. The candidate who flagrantly violates the prevailing faculty views on a sensitive issue will find that academic distinction is insufficient for academic progress.

Academic freedom has looked outward: it has sought to prevent outsiders, be they politicians or trustees, from interfering in the intellectual process. Academic freedom has not looked inward: it has not sought to protect the individual scholar from the pressures of his fellow professors. The much-admired statement on tenure by the American Association of University Professors (I am not one of its admirers) is directed exclusively to ensuring that as soon as possible the young professor will be insulated from the control of the university administration and the students, but it neglects the powerful and continuing sanctions possessed by that professor's colleagues.

It has gradually become evident to members of the academic community that this community imposes sharp limits on the range of respectable opinion within its ranks. When a nearly unanimous majority of the prominent professors are on one side, whether it be a war, the exit of Jews from Russia, the progressive income tax, or the busing of students, it creates a suspicion that disinterested scholarship is not the only academic value in the selection of faculty. Why then, if the great majority of the faculty is opposed to some powerful group in the society, should that group fail to counterattack with whatever political weapons it can find?

My complaint should not be misunderstood or exaggerated. There is no conspiracy among thousands of faculty members to exclude certain views—it is simply the case that Plato would have a difficult time getting an appointment at a major university if he were, say, an energetic leader of the John Birch society. It is not true that all views are excluded; I am reasonably confident, for example, that I am expressing a viewpoint uncongenial to a majority of my colleagues at the University of Chicago. All important groups in a society succeed in finding intellectuals who will serve as their spokesmen, but many of these groups must search for such people outside the great universities.

I know of one and only one way to reduce coercive power, and that is by dividing it among more holders. American universities probably have a greater toleration for heretical views than English or French or German universities, and if this be so it is not because we are more firmly wedded to intellectual freedom and tolerance but because we have many more high-quality institutions and considerably less centralization of control. The way to increase that toleration for dissent is to divide further the control over our universities.

I urge that we foster the program of diffusion of power in at least two main directions.

First, all public aid to higher education for teaching should be given to students, not to universities. In this age it is fashionable to ridicule the capacities of all consumers, students among them. I firmly believe, on the contrary, that students possess the ability, the access to knowledge, and above all the self-interest to seek out and patronize the institutions, the subjects, and the teachers best suited to their interests. We already have immense variety in our institutions, so a student with general tuition-purchasing power could choose from an array ranging from our great universities to Dutch Elm College, where an A.B. in mathematics certifies 90 percent accuracy in knowledge of the multiplication table. I argue for extending this freedom within each institution to the maximum that is compatible with the honest labeling of degrees. Some of the main innovations in higher education in America have come from student demands and student supports, and these contributions will increase if students are given direct control over public expenditures on instruction.

This dangerous proposal for what the economist calls "consumer sovereignty" should be carried much further than untying public assistance from specific institutions. I believe that a substantial portion of the income of a teacher should depend upon the fees he can garner from students. The wonderful effect of income upon attention and energy, which Adam Smith remarked on over two centuries ago, would assure an entirely new level of teaching performance in American universities.

The second direction of reform should be in the area of research: the process of disbursing research funds should also be decentralized and made as competitive as possible. If the laws against monopoly and undue concentration have value (and I believe they have value), the value is at its greatest in areas that influence men's minds. The case for competition is stronger in scholarship than it is in bread.

Yet we have been moving steadily toward increased concentration of control over research funds. A few great foundations have immense power over the directions of research, and I would urge that severe limits be put upon the size of any one foundation. The federal government is now not only the greatest source of funds for even the richest of private universities, but also is increasingly centralizing its research programs within fewer and more specialized bodies such as the National Science Foundation and the National Institutes of Health. I despair of successfully applying the Sherman Act to the federal government, but even short of that splendid vision there is vast scope for decentralizing the closely knit scientific establishment in Washington.

That is the message. Competition—infinitely diverse and tenacious competition—which already plays a large but hobbled role in American higher education, is the sovereign defense against the pressures toward conformity that threaten to politicize and subvert the university.

TWO

All about Economics

11

Stigler's Law of Demand and Supply Elasticities

I propose the following theorem, which (I hope) is sufficiently significant in its implications and rigorous in its demonstration to deserve the title of "law":

> All demand curves are inelastic, and
> all supply curves are inelastic, too.

I have ventured to attach my name to this law because this will be its first completely explicit formulation and demonstration, although it has long lurked in the background of economic discussion. Both empirical and a priori demonstrations will be given.

Empirical Demonstration

In principle, it is impossible to establish empirically that all of the demand and supply curves that have ever

---

I long delayed publication of this piece for fear that too many readers would find it persuasive. Time and events have probably not affected its truth.

existed or will someday exist are inelastic. Yet it is possible to establish a strong presumption that this is true by showing that, in a wide variety of investigations, elastic functions are conspicuous by their absence.

I begin with academic investigations, and necessarily my list of examples is insultingly incomplete, because editors' demands for brevity are also inelastic. First I shall report a few statistical findings; these deserve little weight because (aside from many technical weaknesses) almost always only short-run functions are derived.

Henry Schultz: "With the possible exception of buckwheat (first and third periods), and of rye for the third period, the demand for all the ten commodities [sugar, corn, cotton, hay, wheat, potatoes, oats, barley, rye, and buckwheat] is inelastic (i.e., $/\eta/ < 1$)." *Theory and Measurement of Demand* (Chicago: University of Chicago Press, 1938), p. 556.

David A. Wells: "A further analysis of the experiences of the New York and Brooklyn Bridge since its construction also reveals some curious tendencies of the American people in respect to consumption and expenditures ... In the third year, with a reduction of foot-fares to one-fifth of a cent [from one cent], the number of foot-passengers declined 440,395, or to an aggregate of 3,239,-337; while the number of car-passengers (with a reduction of fare from five to two and a half cents) increased 10,130,957, or to 21,843,250." *Recent Economic Changes* (New York: Appleton, 1889), pp. 386–387.

E. H. Schoenberg: "The coefficient of elasticity [of demand for cigarettes] at the means is −0.68." "The Demand Curve for Cigarettes," *Journal of Business* 6 (January 1933): 35.

E. J. Broster: "The elasticities of demand for tea are 0.554 with respect to price and 0.284 with respect to income." "Elasticities of Demand for Tea and Price-Fixing Policy," *Review of Economic Studies* 6 (June 1939): 169.

R. M. Walsh: "The elasticity of supply for cotton acreage varied from 0.1 to 0.3 at different levels of price." "Response to Price in Production of Cotton and Cottonseed," *Journal of Farm Economics* 26 (May 1944): 372.

Much weightier is the testimony of economists, who eschew mechanical calculation and carefully combine all the relevant information:

Alvin H. Hansen: "But most industries are confronted, at best, with a unit elasticity of demand." *Fiscal Policy and Business Cycles* (New York: Norton, 1941), p. 326.

A. Walters: "Demand on the copper market has always been fairly inelastic." "The International Copper Cartel," *Southern Economic Journal* 11 (October 1944): 143.

J. H. Jones: "If, however, we refer to the general demand [for coal] of the world as a whole, . . . it is undoubtedly true to say that it is inelastic." "The Present Position of the British Coal Trade," *Journal of the Royal Statistical Society,* 93, pt. 1 (1930): 10.

A. Abrahamson: "High whiskey prices may have some slight effect in discouraging consumption." *Price and Price Policies,* ed. W. Hamilton (New York: McGraw-Hill, 1938), p. 427.

L. H. Seltzer: "The consumers' demand for credit is relatively insensitive to ordinary changes in interest rates." "Is a Rise in Interest Rates Desirable or Inevitable?" *American Economic Review* 35 (December 1945): 837.

G. J. Stigler: "One is struck by the narrow range of fluctuation of consumption, which certainly argues for an unusually inelastic demand [for wheat in the United Kingdom, 1890–1904]." Notes on the History of the Giffen Paradox," *Journal of Political Economy* 55 (April 1947): 154–155.

J. K. Eastman: "The demand for tin is highly inelastic over most of the price range experienced in recent years." "Rationalisation in the Tin Industry," *Review of Economic Studies* 4 (October 1936): 13.

R. B. Shuman: "But within the usual experience range, there is no evidence that a shift of a few cents a gallon [of gasoline] has any material effect on sales." *The Petroleum Industry* (Norman: University of Oklahoma Press, 1940), p. 144.

W. H. Nicholls: "Agriculture is particularly vulnerable in [an unstable] economy, because (1) it maintains production even in the face of ruinously low prices." "A Price Policy for Agriculture, Consistent with Economic Progress, that Will Promote Adequate and More Stable Income from Farming," *Journal of Farm Economics* 27 (November 1945): 744.

This list of demonstrations by academic students could be continued indefinitely, but now I must turn briefly to the business community:

Steel: "The demand for steel is very inelastic." U.S. Steel Corporation, *Temporary National Economic Committee Papers*, vol. 1, p. 169.

Cement: "I never found that the company who made those reductions in price obtained any benefit from it whatsoever. If they reduced the price they might have gotten one particular contract, ... but, in the end, they got no more business." President Brobston of Hercules Cement, *333 U.S. Supreme Court Briefs and Records 683–740*, vol. 2 (1947), pp. 7697–98.

Automobiles: "I do not consider that the present price level of automobiles will have any material bearing on the industry over the twelve months' period. Without question, the prices as announced at the shows were rather a shock to the automobile purchasing public ... The objection to price will level itself off within a very short time." A sales manager, *Automotive Industries*, December 4, 1937, p. 811.

Indigo: "An increase in price by all suppliers would undoubtedly disabuse the buyers' minds of the impression now general that an indigo price reduction is imminent and to this extent would greatly strengthen present demand." Mitsui Trading Company, Hearings on S2303, Senate Committee on Patents, 77th Cong., 2d Sess., p. 2380.

For the most comprehensive and authoritative information, however, one must turn to the experience of men who have controlled large sectors of the economy. Before the war was over, the Office of Price Administration had characterized almost all salable things in the American economy, except economists' services, in terms such as these:

"The increased use of southern pine lumber stemming from the defense program and the accompanying expanded economic activity has caused demand to exceed supply [sic]. As a consequence, inflationary pressure has caused prices to rise greatly in excess of previously existing industry levels." Price Schedule no. 19, November 24, 1941, p. 1.

"As a result of the much increased demand and the temptation to speculation which this has provided, prices of cattle tail hair and winter hog hair have shown sharp increases which are not warranted by any increase in cost of production and which can have little effect in augmenting the supply." Price Schedule no. 24, August 27, 1941, p. 1.

Of course, some of these passages could be interpreted as meaning that the demand curve had merely shifted far to the right, and was not necessarily inelastic. But a variety of ancillary considerations oppose this interpretation. The uses of subsidies and differential prices usually rested on inelasticity of supply. The use of allocations, rationing, and priorities rested on inelasticities of demand. Every price rise was "unwarranted"; but the warrant of a price rise is to encourage supply and/or ration demand; hence, the OPA economists meant that higher prices would fail to perform these functions. Moreover, when pressed they will concede that price control was successful because it kept down index numbers of prices—that is, it had no appreciable effects on output.

And finally, let us look to Great Britain where, economic events being centrally planned, all supply and demand functions were known. Here the evidence of ubiquitous inelasticity is silently impressive: in the economic plan (as reported in the *Economic Survey* for 1948), no reference is made to relative prices. For example, "In the United States we are making great efforts to increase our exports, but any really large expansion would require a radical change in the importing habits of that country" (p. 10). That is, lower prices would not increase American dollar purchases. Again, in dealing with excess peak demand for electricity, several devices are alluded to as possible solutions (pp. 24–26), but no reference is made to raising rates, which therefore must be ineffective. All in all, this—one may say deliberate and systematic—disregard of prices is powerful evidence for the law.

I therefore consider the empirical evidence overwhelming. Of course elastic demands have sometimes been alleged, usually without any real evidence. But in at least two cases, evidence of a sort has been proffered:

Cranberry sauce: "Assuming income per head at the preceding year's level, the market can be expected to absorb every year a 17.5 percent increase in the quantity of cranberry sauce marketed, without a decline in price. Every percent increase in quantity *in excess of 17.5 percent* over the previous year would *depress* the price by 0.49 percent below the previous year's level." C. D. Hyson and F. H. Sanderson, "Monopolistic Discrimination in the Cranberry Industry," *Quarterly Journal of Economics* 59 (1944–45): 348, 350.

Domestic servants: "The price elasticity . . . has an even greater absolute value: −2.3. G. J. Stigler, *Domestic Servants in the United States, 1900–40* (New York: National Bureau of Economic Research, 1947), pp. 30, 32.

These adverse examples are not necessarily proof of the ineptitude of the investigators: they can be explained very simply as the result of Sampling Fluctuations.

A Priori Demonstration

I shall give two proofs that all demand curves are inelastic. Each covers most of the economy; the two together surely cover all industries once and most industries twice. But I do not wish to purchase elegance with uncertainty. Thereafter the elasticity of supply will be examined.

First, Alfred Marshall's proof: "The third condition [for inelastic demand] is that only a small part of the expenses of production of the commodity should consist of the price of this factor. Since the plasterer's wages are but a small part of the total expenses of building a house, a rise of even 50 percent in them would add but a very small percentage to the expenses of production of a house and would check demand but little." *Principles of Economics* (New York: Macmillan, 1920), p. 385.

Now, almost every product is a small part of the expense of some other product: steel accounts for only a tenth of the cost of an automobile; transportation charges are a small part of delivered prices; the cost of a home is a small part of the cost of living. Thus, most demand curves are inelastic.[1] It may be noted that Marshall assumed for purposes of this argument that no substitution is possible among the various inputs. Who can question his right to do this?

Second, the expectation proof. When prices rise, no

1. This proof has an august corollary. Since most or all specific costs of production are relatively small, and entrepreneurs do not bother with small costs, therefore they do not bother with costs at all. Hence they do not maximize profits. This corollary has implications for economic theory.

one will buy less of commodities, because prices are expected to rise further; and when prices fall, no one buys more, because prices are expected to fall further. The anticipation of purchases when prices rise, and the postponement of purchases when prices fall, serve to confirm and continue the expectations. (Some economists go on to say that the way to decrease quantity demanded—and increase quantity supplied—is to lower prices, but this may be making too much of a good thing.)

No one can question the general validity of this proof, but in this—its usual—form it lacks refinement and rigor. The first price change does not set off the anticipations; clearly it was also anticipated. And a seller anticipates in the case of price reductions, for example, that the first reduction would simply confirm buyers' anticipations and not help sales, so he may make the reduction in two steps to eliminate anticipation of further decreases. But, of course, the buyers can easily anticipate this. So the seller cuts the price exactly the amount they anticipated, just to get it over with; but this they did not anticipate, so business deteriorates. The seller never anticipated this result, so in panic he makes an unanticipated further price change, and at this, business naturally comes to a halt. After certain further, obvious steps, which I shall omit for brevity's sake, price eventually settles down. Sales resume—at the old rate, it is to be anticipated.

The careful reader will have noticed that supply has received little attention; this gap will now be filled. The fact is, that inelastic demands imply inelastic supplies; hence, it is sufficient to prove the existence of the former. Some economists are so inconsistent as to say that demands are inelastic but that marginal cost curves are horizontal. The following proof will show that this is ill-advised.

First, an intuitive proof. If the demand for input A is inelastic, a 10 percent decrease in its price leads to less than a 10 percent increase in the quantity taken; and similarly for other inputs. If all input prices decrease 10 percent, an even smaller increase in the quantity of A that is taken will occur, for substitution incentives disappear; and similarly for other inputs. But a fall of 10 percent in the price of each input is equivalent to a rise of (about) 11 percent in the price of product. Therefore an 11 percent rise in the price of the product leads to less than a 10 percent increase of each input, and therefore to less than a 10 percent increase of output, so supply is inelastic. This proof is deficient in that it glosses over the possibility of extreme complementarity of inputs; the deficiency will be removed mathematically.

Let us define some symbols:

$$x = \text{output,}$$
$$a, b = \text{inputs,}$$
$$p, p_a, p_b = \text{respective prices,}$$
$$x = \phi\,(a,\ b) = \text{production function.}$$

The conditions for maximum profit are,

$$p\phi_a = p_a; \qquad p\phi_b = p_b.$$

Differentiate these equations partially with respect to p_a, and then with respect to p_b, and define the symbols:

$$\Delta = \begin{vmatrix} \phi_{aa} & \phi_{ab} \\ \phi_{ab} & \phi_{bb} \end{vmatrix},$$

$$\eta_a = \frac{\partial a}{\partial p_a} \frac{p_a}{a},$$

$$\eta_b = \frac{\partial b}{\partial p_b} \frac{p_b}{b},$$

$$\eta_{ab} = \frac{\partial b}{\partial p_a} \frac{p_a}{b}.$$

Then

$$\eta_a = p_a \phi_{bb}/ap\Delta,$$

$$\eta_b = p_b \phi_{aa}/bp\Delta,$$
$$\eta_{ab} = - p_a \phi_{ab}/bp\Delta.$$

Now differentiate the maximum profit equations with respect to p, to obtain,

$$\frac{\partial a}{\partial p} = (p_b \phi_{ab} - p_a \phi_{bb})/p^2\Delta,$$

$$\frac{\partial b}{\partial p} = (p_a \phi_{ab} - p_b \phi_{aa})/p^2\Delta.$$

Finally, the elasticity of supply is

$$\eta_s = \frac{\partial x}{\partial p} \frac{p}{x} = \frac{p}{x}(\phi_a \frac{\partial a}{\partial p} + \phi_b \frac{\partial b}{\partial p}).$$

If one substitutes around a bit, and defines k_a as ap_a/xp, and similarly for k_b, one will reach this equation:

$$\eta_s = k_a|\eta_a| + k_b|\eta_b| - 2k_b\eta_{ab}.$$

Recall that we have shown that $|\eta_a| < 1$, $|\eta_b| < 1$. The implications are unambiguous. First, if $\eta_{ab} > 0$ (inputs are substitutes), then

$$\eta_s < 1, \text{ for } k_a|\eta_a| + k_b|\eta_b| < 1.$$

Second, if perchance $\eta_{ab} < 0$, we notice that if $\Delta > 0$, as stability of equilibrium recommends, then

$$k_a \eta_a \eta_b > k_b \eta_{ab}^2.$$

At worst, therefore,

$$\eta_s < (\sqrt{k_a |\eta_a|} + \sqrt{k_b |\eta_b|})^2$$

But the expression on the right can be assumed, with no loss of specificity, to be less than unity.

Q.E.D.

Implications

The terminological implication is that demands and supplies with elasticities of zero should be called inelastic; those with elasticities numerically less than unity, elastic. Elasticity has the same range of variation as the coefficient of correlation, correctly calculated.

The discussion of the economic implications must be reserved for another occasion, when it will be shown that there is no price system.

12

On Scientific Writing

In the September 1947 issue of the *American Economic Review*, Alvin Hansen states: "Of the $60 billion gross capital formation in business plant and equipment made in the decade 1931–40, 90 percent was replacement investment" (p. 563). His colleague Seymour Harris, writing in the August 1947 issue of the *Review of Economic Statistics*, states: "But let us not forget that for the decade of the thirties, gross investment was but $60 billion and *net* investment was approximately zero" (p. 152). The comparison suggests at least four comments:

1. The same figure is given for two rather different series; business capital is only part of total capital.
2. The amount of net investment differs.

This letter to an admired friend proposed a method of raising the technical quality of professional writing. He accepted its feasibility, and I still do, but I was unattracted by the task. I owe apologies to the late Professor Hansen for choosing his work as an example, especially since some of mine would serve as well!

3. Neither man gives any reference for his figures.
4. The probable source is the Department of Commerce, which has no series with these titles. The most plausible series do not approximate Hansen's $60 billion, or his 90 percent.

This almost studied carelessness in the use of facts is very common in economic literature. It is not necessary, or even proper, for me to emphasize to a perfectionist like you the objections to this sort of work. There may be deception. If these errors are widespread and increasing, we may have to give up division of labor. In any event, such errors are more than a symptom of general sloppiness of thought and research procedures—they are an integral part of that sloppiness. Nor do I need to argue the desirability of improving the quality of economic research and writing.

I believe that real improvements could be obtained by checking a large range of economic literature and publishing the results of the checking. Let me spell out this proposal.

The Types of Error

Economists possess their full share of the common ability to invent and commit errors: copying a number wrong, forgetting to tell what number it is or where they got it, making arithmetical mistakes, relying upon fickle memory, and so on. They can reason fallaciously, with or without mathematics. They can misread completely the state of affairs, or reverse the direction of causation. Perhaps their most common error is to believe other economists.

It is impossible to check thoroughly the quality of economic literature, even on a narrow front. Even the most competent economist will be biased in what he checks: he will accept as true the statements or bits of reasoning that he believes and he will examine with critical care the views that are novel or contradictory to those he has been holding. Moreover, there is no ultimate test of validity: even the history of mathematics is studded with universally accepted errors.

Checks of the quality of economic literature should be relatively free of ambiguity as to both what is to be checked, and whether it is correct or erroneous. Two types of material seem capable of fairly large-scale and objective measurement of accuracy: statements of empirical fact and quotations from other writers. Of course, one must make concessions to the more or less legitimate desire of an economist to be read. There is no point in checking, or trying to check, (1) sweeping generalizations (capitalism is dying); (2) widely accepted beliefs (a depression started in 1929); (3) the completeness of references to well known sources or series (the cost-of-living index need not be referred to as compiled by the Bureau of Labor Statistics, referring to clerical and manual workers in 85 large American cities, and so on). Nor would I attempt to check paraphrases of the writings of other people, except where specific numbers are involved, since arguable points arise immediately.

The checking of fairly specific statements seems to me eminently useful for two reasons. First, it is not probable that a man who is careless in small matters is careful in large ones; quite the contrary, a man who cannot even copy a sentence of Keynes's correctly is not likely to be a reliable reporter of complicated or badly expressed ideas. Second, it is precisely in these narrower matters that the reader is most at the writer's mercy: a reputable economist, writing in a reputable journal, acquires an aura of reliability, and after all, we cannot check many things and still do our own work.

The Measurement of Errors

I propose that all of the leading American economic journals for some recent year be used as the basis of the tests. This ensures variety of authorship and subject, and permits no invidious selection. A group of graduate students could subject each empirical statement and quotation to verification, given suitable training and supervision. I have not explored the problem sufficiently to have very definite ideas on the nature of the tests, but two examples suggest their general nature.

Empirical statements. Hansen, in the article referred to above, makes sixteen distinct statements of a specific nature about prices and capital formation. Among the relevant tests are:

1. Frequency and accuracy of source. He gives no sources.
2. Adequacy of description. One series—retail food prices—is adequately described; "prices" refers to wholesale prices; "finished goods prices" is a title abandoned years ago for "manufactured goods

prices"; and his capital formation series is ambiguous.
3. Frequency of error. Eight of his sixteen statements are wrong.

Possibly something could also be done on the magnitude of error. In Hansen's article, for example, three of the eight errors exceeded 5 percent of the correct figure.

Quotations. I take Marshall's *Principles* (1920) because of its great importance, despite the fact that it was written in an age of more informal scholarship. Of 107 quotations of English sources which were traced, only fifty were correct (or deviated only in punctuation or detail). Of the fifty-seven incorrect quotations, two (both from Adam Smith!) departed in a significant degree from the original. Only seventy-two of the 107 citations of sources could be considered remotely adequate.

In articles based on calculations, it would be possible to assess the adequacy of the descriptions, and the accuracy of the results. But a complete verification of a year's work would be a very large task indeed, and perhaps some sampling would be called for.

The Benefits of the Study

The benefits of such a study, duly publicized, appear to me to be several and substantial.

First, economists will be taught a decent caution as readers. We are all too prone to accept unquestioningly the printed word or number.

Second, there would be an immediate improvement in the low editorial standards of most of our journals. Every editor would edit with more care and demand more adequate references.

Third, the tests will remind economists that footnotes are not an occasional token of respect for an obsolete and purposeless tradition. It will come as a shock to many, I am sure, even to realize that references can be checked.

Fourth, the study may lead to improvement in the quality of training of graduate students. Most teachers are unaware of the problem of quality, so naturally their students are, too. Indeed, the checking of references may become a standard pastime of malicious graduate students—which would be more useful to the students and the profession than the activities of malicious graduate students as I partook in them.

I would be very interested in your opinion of the feasibility and desirability of such a project.

13

How to Pass Examinations in Economics

Students always display a powerful, not to say unhealthy, interest in how to answer questions on examinations in economics. They can do fairly well with the essay, or subjective, questions, but they do not seem at home with the true-false, or objective, questions. And yet the latter questions are very easy. I shall illustrate the proper techniques by using questions from the *Students Manual to Accompany the Elements of Economics* by Lorie Tarshis, by Lorie Tarshis and Phillip Cartwright.[1] Sooner or later, able students will discover that the appendix to the manual gives the answers to the true-false questions (which are called comprehension tests); so it will save time if I reproduce the answers with the questions.

---

1. That is, the book is by Tarshis: Lorie Tarshis, *The Elements of Economics* (Boston: Houghton Mifflin, 1947); the manual is by Tarshis and Cartwright: Lorie Tarshis and Phillip Cartwright, *Students Manual to Accompany the Elements of Economics* (Boston: Houghton Mifflin, 1948). Of course, the manual is a book, too.

This ancient piece is included only because careless students may be thus enticed to buy this volume.

It is very important that the student gain self-confidence, so I shall begin with a simple example:

9. Taxes constitute a part of fixed costs. (Answer: F)[2]

The indicated answer of F is, of course, T. It is important to note that this answer has a very general validity—for example:

9a. Taxes do not constitute a part of fixed costs. (Answer: F)
9b. Taxes constitute a part of variable costs. (Answer: F)
9c. Taxes do not constitute a part of variable costs. (Answer: F)

Every cost, it must be remembered, is fixed or variable, and not both simultaneously. A tax is a cost. But some taxes vary with output and some do not, and the statement refers to tax*es* in the plural. This means that perhaps both fixed and variable taxes are being referred to. Hence, the statement is partly right, part of the time, and therefore false.

Lesson 1: A Statement That *Can* Be False *Is* False.

Since we are on the subject of taxes, let us tackle the next question, which is rather more difficult:

10. A tax on corporation profits is a variable cost. (Answer: F)

The student could easily fall into a trap of his own construction here. He might reason: the corporation tax

2. Ibid., p. 17. F means fantastic.

varies with the corporation's profits, and the profits vary with output, so the corporation tax varies with output.

Lesson 2: A Tax on Corporation Profits Is Not a Variable Cost.

Now that self-confidence has been gained, it is necessary to acquire humility:

6. If firms do not seek to maximize profits, their output will not be that at which the marginal cost and revenue are equal. (Answer: T)[3]

The lads who think they are clever will argue: If the firm doesn't care about profits, might it not accidentally operate at this output? And according to Lesson 1, that would make the statement false. But let's see where such superficial cleverness leads. Such a student will feel impelled to answer the following question as follows:

6a. If firms seek not to maximize profits, their output will not be that at which the marginal cost and revenue are equal (Answer: T—but really F)

For one thing, marginal cost equals marginal revenue also at minimum profits. For another thing, a firm can make a mistake, can't it? To return to the original question, everything is a matter of probability. There are many possible outputs, and probably only one maximizes profits. Besides, profits usually aren't maximized when marginal cost equals (total) revenue.

Lesson 3: A Statement That *Can* Be True *Is* True.

3. Ibid., p. 44. T means theoretically.

In preparing for an examination in economics, it is desirable to study the economy for years and thus acquire a feel for the facts. See how realistic insight helps on this one:

7. If a tax of three cents per unit is imposed on the product of a perfectly competitive industry, the price will rise by exactly three cents. (Answer: F)[4]

This statement is false for three reasons: there are no perfectly competitive industries; if there were, they would not be constant-cost industries; and if they were, they wouldn't raise the price of a locomotive by just three cents.

Lesson 4: Know Your Economy.

Even a good student will sometimes overlook a section of the economy or the textbook. Even so, formal logic may come to his rescue:

10. Although theoretically the control of a corporation is vested in all of its owners, in actual fact the control of most corporations rests with their elected directors. (Answer: T)[5]

Remember page 58: "Theory and practice should not contradict one another." So if in theory the owners control the corporation, then in fact they do; if in fact the directors control the corporations, then in theory they do.

4. Ibid., p. 62.
5. Ibid., p. 11. Tarshis, or Tarshis and Cartwright, are probably the only economists who have studied the distribution of control in the hundreds of thousands of corporations. T or F?

Hence, owners and directors are identical. Once we know this, the answer follows directly.

Lesson 5: Know Your Logic.

I now turn to Keynesian economics, one of the more difficult branches of economic theory. I begin with a troublesome question:

1. If prices are inflexible, an increase in the wage rates paid by one firm will not lead it to dismiss employees. (Answer: T)[6]

The key to this question is that wages rise only for one firm. Hence this firm hires kinds of labor that no other firm hires (unless it is being discriminated against, cruelly). If it did fire any workers, where could they go? The entrepreneur is a decent chap.

Lesson 6: Not Every Entrepreneur Is Greedy.

Of course, some Keynesian economics is very simple. For example:

1. If investment rises from forty to forty-five and then remains steady at forty-five, the national income will rise very rapidly and then rise at a slower rate. (Answer: F)[7]

This is very easy, and indeed I put it in merely as a breather before the next question. Since it required

6. Ibid., p. 124.
7. ibid., p. 98.

eighty-seven years and three months for investment to rise from forty just to forty-one, why should the national income rise very rapidly?

Lesson 7: Read and Write Carefully.

Now I come to a question that has the full flavor of the Keynesian theory:

7. Neglecting the acceleration effects, public investment directed to useless projects enriches the country. (Answer: T)[8]

Since I have not read this chapter of Tarshis' book, I do not know his precise explanation. No doubt it is very similar to mine: governments are so foolish that they are more likely to do good when they don't try than when they do. This reminds me that an economist named Sir Roy Harrod recently wrote a pamphlet in which he argued that a country (named England) was getting impoverished because there was too much useful public investment. Oddly enough, Harrod (who wrote the official life of Keynes) claims that Keynes would agree with him!

Lesson 8: Not Everybody Understands Keynesian Economics.

8. Ibid., p. 115. It also enriches the city.

Finally, I want to emphasize how important it is for the student to keep his wits about him:

4. Farmers suffer as much in depression as do wage earners. (Answer: T—but really F)[9]

The wrong answer was given in the appendix, I am sure, to see if the student had been lulled into a state of uncritical receptiveness. It stands to reason that farmers do not suffer as much as do wage earners. For one thing, there aren't as many farmers. For another thing, it is not very probable that farmers suffer *exactly* as much as wage earners.

Lesson 9: Nobody Knows the Suffering That Farmers (and Students) Do.

9. Ibid., p. 88.

14

The Alarming Cost of Model Changes: A Case Study

Franklin Fisher, Zvi Griliches, and Carl Kaysen have shown, in an article which will command wide and respectful attention, that if consumers had been content with the 1949 automobile, they would be saving over $700 per car by 1961.[1] They properly have left open the question of whether improvements such as greater speeds and automatic transmissions were worth the cost; but after all, the 1949 cars ran, and kept out the rain.[2] The $5 billion a year of extra costs had better alternative uses—paying higher tuition fees perhaps, or providing more adequate farm subsidies, or a violin in every home.

Their choice of the automobile industry was arbitrary,

1. "The Costs of Automobile Model Changes since 1949," *Journal of Political Economy* 70 (October 1962): 433–461.
2. My 1950 Dodge was considerably more efficient in the latter role than in the former, however.

Vulgar luxury has always been condemned by men of high taste and income. Economists have lent some support to their displeasure, and I add my mite.

but reasonable: there has been much comment on over-elaborate automobiles; it is a large industry; and annual model changes are a prominent feature of its behavior. Of course, every sector—even public schools and health—displays a mixture of frivolous and genuine improvements; and eventually, let us hope, estimates of the costs of product changes will be available for all. I propose here to estimate the costs for another industry—publishing—in which the frequency of model changes has reached an almost unbelievable pitch.

The publishing industry attracted my attention when I undertook to compare various editions of the same work. It is essentially correct that a man never changes, and seldom improves on, his views: certainly this is true of David Ricardo (three editions), J. S. Mill (seven editions), Alfred Marshall (eight editions), Eugen von Böhm-Bawerk (three editions), Léon Walras (five editions), Arthur Pigou (four editions), Wilhelm Roscher (twenty-seven editions), and so on. I suspect that the revision of textbooks every five years reflects market considerations more than it expresses the march of scientific progress. The costs of this sort of minor amendment are not negligible—unlike the automobile, the older editions lose their usefulness.

But the phenomenon of change goes much deeper. Each year about 11,000 books are published in the United States. Not *one* would make the list of the 100 greatest books of all time. Why must we have the *Rise and Fall of the Third Reich,* when the *Rise and Fall of the Dutch Republic* is a better book, and in the public domain? Is *Tropic of Cancer* better (worse) than the works of the Marquis de Sade? What, precisely, are the respects in which Tennessee Williams surpasses Shakespeare? Paul Samuelson [1963] (five editions), G. L. Bach (three editions), Lowell Harriss (four editions), and others write economics textbooks. Is it abundantly clear that they are better books than *The Wealth of Nations?*

The economist cannot answer these questions. The answers rest on value judgments, which are not scientific, and the economist is a scientist. All the economist can do is report the facts. As Fisher, Griliches, and Kaysen say, we cannot tell a drunkard to stop drinking, but we can audit the bar bill. Or, to choose a metaphor without normative overtones, we cannot tell a nation to stop turning beautiful trees into waste paper, but we can weigh the ashes.

So let us assume that no new books were printed after 1900. This date is less arbitrary than 1949, I think, and in any event it yields bigger numbers. Some books of this earlier period would probably sell in only small quantities (I have in mind an item such as J. S. Mill's *An Examination of Sir William Hamilton's Philosophy, and of the Principal Philosophical Questions Discussed in His Writings;* or Sir John Sinclair's twenty-one-volume survey of Scotland in 1791–1799), although without the diversion of the new models their markets would strengthen. Some books might even disappear (I have in mind such an item as Heinrich's *Phlogiston ist die Wahrheit*). But there would be an ample selection of reading matter: the books of 1900 and before could not run or keep out the rain, but they could furnish the minds of Newton, Gauss, Beethoven, and Goethe, of Jefferson and Lincoln and Dred Scott.

The stream of savings would be immense, and it would

be fed by a thousand hidden springs. Let me just cite four important components.

First, all books would be royalty free, with savings of perhaps 10 percent on retail prices. The authors would usually have alternative products.

Second, the plates of a typical book now print about 3,000 copies. This could be raised to at least 200,000 with a reduction of 98.5 percent in composition costs. Prices would be reduced easily another 30 percent. (This item alone exceeds the savings in the automobile study, as a percent of price.)

Third, advertising of books would fall, perhaps by 98 percent. This would cut prices another 5 or 10 percent.

Fourth, in happy analogy to Fisher, Griliches, and Kaysen, books would get more mileage. Once a family outside Wisconsin grew up, its sturdily bound McGuffy Readers could be passed on to a second generation, and possibly a third. This would reduce costs by a factor of 2.5, making the aggregate saving perhaps 85 percent of present costs.

I shall not pause to estimate indirect savings: houses could be smaller; people would not have to change the prescription of their glasses so often; teachers would not have to think up new examination questions; and so forth.

When we turn to newspapers, the savings would be even greater. There is nothing new under the sun, so it would be sufficient to print a dozen volumes of news once and for all: crimes, wars, women, colonies, frontier life, emancipation, and the Irish Question, for example. In addition to a saving of, say, 98 percent on newspapers, there would be a substantial reduction in efforts by people to get into the news.

These savings are to be calculated in the billions of dollars, and the billions of hours of reader time. There would be some delay in the dissemination of new knowledge—few changes are without costs. I would beg the reader, however, to keep two facts in mind: most new knowledge is false; and the news got around in Athens.

15

Elementary Economic Education

The task force appointed by the American Economic Association and financed by the Committee for Economic Development has reported on the problem of instruction in economics in the high school.[1] The task force contained five highly esteemed economists—G. L. Bach (chairman), Lester Chandler, R. A. Gordon, Ben Lewis, and Paul Samuelson; as well as two specialists in secondary education—Arno Bellack and M. L. Frankel. Although the American Economic Association does not explicitly endorse the report, it chose the economists and hence vouched for their competence and distinction. No other body concerned with economic education has had such professional status, nor is an equally authoritative

1. *Economic Education in the Schools* (New York: Committee for Economic Development, 1961).

The report of the task force created by the American Economic Association to improve the teaching of economics in the high school will become an important influence on our school system. These critical remarks were prepared for a symposium on the report.

body likely to appear soon. The report will therefore command an audience of unusual size and deference among high school and college teachers.

This unusual status is, I believe, unfortunate. The economists composing the task force are leaders in American economics, of unquestionable competence and integrity. But they do not monopolize these virtues, and the mode by which they were selected serves to give their views an eminence that is incompatible with the doctrine of free competition (meaning free discussion) in educational and scientific work. The views of the task force will receive a respectful but critical reading by professional economists; they will not receive anything like so critical a scrutiny by the people in charge of elementary economic education. If—to use an unbelievably remote possibility—I or some other professional reviewer convicted them of error, the important audience would never learn of it.

To this lament on professional sponsorship there is a clear and weighty response. If there is not an authoritative professional influence on high school instruction in economics, what other sources of influence will prevail? The answer is: a strange medley of (1) teachers and school administrators long on pedagogy and short on economics, (2) special-interest groups that flood our schools with variously slanted materials, and (3) a rearguard of textbook salesmen and opinionated local school board members. And has not this strange and not always open competition led to a generally unsatisfactory neglect and/or treatment of economics in the high school?

I have no counterresponse to offer. I even believe that the task force's schemes are better, according to almost every economist's values, than those that now on average prevail. It is for each person to decide whether benevolent monopoly is ever justifiable in the realm of education. My own preference is clear: of all monopolies, that of opinions is the worst.

Let us abandon this question, and look at two other problems that the report raises. The first concerns policy slant; the second concerns pedagogical feasibility.

Readers will know that the report has already been criticized—by the conservative press—as absurdly neutral toward communism and filled with soft welfare-state views. They can conjecture—as I do, since I missed *The Daily Worker* that day—that the other extreme thinks the task force sold out to Wall Street.

I do not propose to discuss the political slant of the report in any detail. It is fair to say that the committee that wrote the report does not include a representative of the extreme 10 percent of economists at each end of the distribution of economists—neither fervent free-market disciples nor extreme interventionists were represented. Since the committee consisted of men who are representative of the central range of professional opinion, one can hardly call its position unrepresentative.

This does not mean that the report is in any sense "impartial"; indeed, I do not know anyone who is impartial or, if he is, how we can know it. I strongly disagree, for example, with the implicit verdict of the task force (and presumably of the profession) that although the problems posed by monopoly deserve extensive discussion (pp. 33–36), no comparable issues are raised by public regulation (p. 36). But obviously neither a Professor Bach nor I can presently persuade the other that he is wrong, or—being honest men—we would have resolved our differences earlier. The only legitimate complaint—and I promise not to recur to this point—is that some (representative) views have been given preferential status among noneconomists.

Let us turn finally to what the task force believes should be in the high school course in economics: "The minimal understanding needed for effective citizenship in the modern American economy" (p. 22). Here full quotation is essential, but the reader will find it sufficient to sample the list. Only their explicit demands for inclusion of topics are listed, although this rule omits subjects that the task force believes to be very important (see, for example, p. 52), but probably for reasons of elegant variation chose not to introduce with "Students should know . . ."

It is important that students understand the central role which markets and prices play in this process [of selecting the goods to produce and the way in which to produce them]. (p. 28)

Students should have a general picture of the national stock of such resources, and of the way in which this stock has grown over the years. (p. 28)

Students should see that the high American standard of living depends on a combination of all these factors [governing productivity]. (p. 29)

The student should understand the relationships between *saving, investment,* and *capital formation.* (p. 29)

Students should also understand, in broad terms, the *principle of diminishing returns.* (p. 30)

It is important for students to see that there are three main types of participants in economic activity. (p. 30)

Individual freedom of choice is central to the "private enterprise way." It is essential that students understand both what this freedom does and does not mean, and also how a private enterprise economy manages to get its business done when individuals are free to make their own economic decisions. (p. 31)

To comprehend the working of markets, the student must understand the main determinants of demand and supply. (p. 32)

Students should know something of the intent and nature of laws designed to enforce competition, and should understand something of the process by which such legislation is enforced through the courts and federal administrative agencies. (pp. 34–35)

Students should be familiar with these trends [in competition] in a general way and, particularly in their history courses, should have the opportunity to look briefly at the development of trusts, holding companies, and other forms of mergers over the past century. (p. 35)

In connection with corporations, it is desirable for students to have a grasp of a *simple* balance sheet and income statement, reflecting only the four or five major categories in each. (p. 36)

Students should also understand the important function performed by securities exchanges, which permit investors to buy and sell readily securities which have already been issued. (p. 36)

It is important for students to understand that, even in a basically free enterprise economy, governments play a significant role in setting priorities and using resources—that is, in deciding what to produce and how to produce it. (p. 37)

Students should have some impression of the order of magnitude of government spending, which now accounts for over a quarter of the national income. (p. 38)

Students should have a general impression of the major taxes currently used. (p. 39)

It is important that the student be introduced to the study of international economic relations. (p. 39)

Students should be given a brief introduction to the concept of the international balance of payments. (p. 40)

One point that should be emphasized with students is the difference between the *balance of trade* and the *balance of payments.* (p. 41)

Students need to be introduced to the fact that many of our greatest economic problems center around how to obtain stable economic growth, avoiding the excesses of the inflationary booms and depressions. (p. 43)

Students should be familiar with the concept [of gross national product], although technical details should be avoided. (p. 44)

Students need to be impressed with the fact that this element of *dynamic interdependence* is a highly important feature of all money-using, private-enterprise economies. (p. 46)

Students should see that the burden imposed upon the taxpayer by a growing public debt depends largely on how rapidly the national income is rising. (p. 47)

Although students should be introduced to money and banking, it is too much to hope that they can master all of the intricacies about them which are found in college textbooks. (p. 48)

Every informed person should understand how new deposits are created when banks make loans or buy securities, and how deposits are correspondingly reduced when bank loans are repaid or the banks sell securities which they have been holding. (p. 49)

The Federal Reserve can control the reserves of the commercial banks which the latter must keep as backing for the public's deposits. Students need understand in only a very general way how this can be done, by raising or lowering commercial bank reserve requirements and through "open market operations." (p. 50)

Students need to understand that we should not expect monetary management to do things that it cannot do, and that we should not damn it for sins of which it is innocent. (p. 50)

But students should be able to see that if a country loses gold, it is likely (or may even be forced) to tighten credit conditions. (p. 51)

It is important for students to understand the vast difference between conditions here and in the underdeveloped economies, and to appreciate some of the problems such economies face. (p. 53)

Students should understand how money incomes arise out of the sale of productive services by individuals to businesses and governments. Equally important, they should understand that these money incomes provide the means of obtaining "real income"—that is, the goods and services that people buy with their money incomes. (p. 55)

Students should know in broad outline of the distribution of personal incomes in the United States, including their own place in the income structure. (p. 56)

Students should understand that high American wages rest fundamentally on the high productivity of American labor. (p. 57)

Every person should understand something of the role of unions in labor-management relations. (p. 58)

The "farm problem" should be understood broadly by students. (p. 59)

Students should be generally familiar with these various arrangements that directly affect their personal economic security. They should also be able to reason objectively about the economic effects, and hence the desirability from different points of view, of these different types of security measures. (p. 60)

Every informed American should have a general impression of how other types of economic systems operate, especially communism. (p. 61)

In addition to being able to compare private enterprise and communism, the student should also be sensitively aware of the fact that various democratic societies—the United Kingdom, the Scandinavian countries, and India, for example—have chosen to adopt socialism in varying degrees. (p. 63)

Amen!

This list of things a high school student should know is, of course, a representative table of contents of a textbook on elementary economics at the college level. Since high school seniors are slightly less mature and substantially less selected than college freshmen, and since high school economics teachers are appreciably less well trained in economics than instructors of college courses, I take it as rigorously implied that if our present college courses are failing to teach students economics, the proposed high school course will fail by a greater margin.

This is in fact my thesis: the watered-down encyclopedia that constitutes the present course in beginning college economics does not teach the student how to think about economic questions. The brief exposure to each of a vast array of techniques and problems gives the student no basic economic logic with which to analyze the economic questions he will face as a citizen. The student will memorize a few facts, diagrams, and policy recommendations, and ten years later will be as untutored in economics as the day he entered the class.

This is a bold pronouncement, and gains no authority by coming from a teacher who is many years away from his last course in elementary economics. The thesis will be rejected more completely, I believe, by the teachers of elementary economics than by the textbook writers: it is instructive that the successful textbooks keep *adding* subject matter to their successive editions in response to market demands.

But the thesis that our present college courses (and, a fortiori, the proposed high school course) fail to impart any permanently useful economic training runs against faith, not evidence. I propose the following test:

Select a sample of seniors (I would prefer men and women five years out of college), equally divided between those who have never had a course in economics and those who have had a conventional one-year course. Give them an examination on current economic problems—*not* on textbook questions. I predict they will not differ in their performance.

I shall illustrate below the kind of question that should be asked in this test.

An introductory-terminal course in economics makes its greatest contribution to the education of students if it concentrates upon a few subjects, which are developed in sufficient detail and applied to a sufficient variety of actual economic problems to cause the student to absorb the basic logic of the approach. The few subjects should be chosen with a view to their importance (which includes the frequency with which they are encountered) and to what present-day economics has to contribute to their understanding. Both criteria, I believe, argue for an immense concentration on price theory—the allocation of resources and the pricing of goods and services.

It seems almost beyond dispute that the citizen is called upon overwhelmingly, indeed almost exclusively, to pass on policies governing the allocation of resources and the formation of prices. I consider this proposition to be self-evident in the area of state and local governmental policies; and it is hardly less true of national economic problems. I made a more or less complete count of the bills that were passed by the first session of the Eighty-first Congress (1959) to get the following tabulation of bills with a strong or exclusively economic interest:

1. Disposal of national resources and Indian lands; at least seventy-one bills, of which general bills numbered   5
2. Regulation of economic activity
   Agriculture   13
   Merchant Marine   7
   Housing   6
   Highways   6
   Labor   7
   Other: banking, air pollution, imports, and so on   22
3. Taxation (individual taxes)   9
4. Tax exemption   5
5. General appropriation acts   16
6. Selective expenditures
   Salaries   12
   Veterans   11
   Other   29
7. Monetary policy   3

To the extent that the economist has anything to say in these areas, he uses price theory ninety-nine times for every instance in which income and employment theory has any relevance. Questions directed primarily to maintaining employment are posed so infrequently, and are even then (as in the appropriation acts) so completely dominated by allocative questions that for practical purposes they are an infrequent and minor problem for the citizen.

If the elementary course were to recognize the civic preeminence of traditional value and distribution theory, it would spend much less time on other parts of economics. And if it recognized the immense variety of allocation problems, and the impossibility of giving a mastery of detailed techniques to the one-year student, it would concentrate on the essential logic of competition and monopoly, of consumer choice, and of the theory of wages. The student would be taught not elasticities or envelopes or oligopolistic models, but the central issues of analysis and fact in questions such as the following:[2]

HR. 236: To prohibit discrimination because of age in the hiring and employment of persons by government contractors.

HR. 1251: To authorize a five-year program of grants and scholarships for collegiate education in the field of nursing.

HR. 2895: To grant a pension of $100 a month to all honorably discharged veterans of World War I who are over sixty-two years of age.

HR. 5983: To enable producers to provide a supply of turkeys adequate to meet the needs of consumers, to

2. This list is from unsuccessful bills of the first session, Eighty-first Congress, but the headlines of the newspapers would do as well.

maintain orderly marketing conditions, and to promote and expand the consumption of turkeys and turkey products.

HR. 7714:   To define, regulate, and license television service contractors.

HR. 9038:   To amend the Tariff Act of 1930 to provide for the establishment of country-by-country quotas for the importation of shrimps and shrimp products.

S. 215:   To supplement the antitrust laws of the United States by requiring that corporations, in industries so heavily concentrated that monopoly or the threat of monopoly is present, file advance notice and make public justification before effectuating price increases.

I proposed above a test of whether our present elementary courses had any lasting value. The questions that ought to be used in such a test are precisely the current questions of policy. Give the student a summary page or two of the arguments and evidence presented in the discussion (in Congress and the public press) of HR. 5983 (orderly turkeys) and let him explain the benefits and costs of the scheme—with the grading based, of course, on the coherence of his argument and relevance of his evidence, not on the conclusions reached.[3]

Let us hope that the test would reveal that our present

3. Such questions can be preceded by simpler ones, such as that which Senator Stuart Symington recently flunked: If stockpiles of materials owned by the government are given directly to defense contractors rather than sold in the market, will we not be able to dispose of them without depressing their prices?

elementary courses do not have a zero, or negative, value. The test would still leave open the question: Would intense concentration on the basic logic of price theory, applied to two score of real problems, give a vastly better and more lasting training than the current encyclopedic texts? Surely, the answer is yes.

16

The Case, if Any, for Economic Literacy

There is an easy case for economic literacy, and for every other kind of literacy. A man ought to be acquainted with all the great branches of knowledge simply to be an educated person, a rounded man, abreast of his society in its varied lines of literary, scientific, artistic, and behavioral knowledge. In addition to this value judgment, which is shared by all nations, there is a utilitarian argument for general literacy. The citizen of a democracy is called upon to judge public policy in a thousand directions—military, educational, medical, economic, and recreational, for example—and he will make better decisions if he is well-informed.

The difficulty with this general argument for all literacy is suggested by carrying it to its conclusion: Why should not the citizen learn all of human knowledge? He will assuredly be impeccably educated, and well-

A plea for economic literacy that just possibly is self-serving advice from an economist.

equipped to discharge his civic duties. Never was a reply easier to find: no one is able to learn all knowledge— man's limited learning capacities and his limited length of life are enough to prevent him from becoming a professional economist, a physician, a concert pianist, a tennis champion, and a federal judge. Indeed he cannot even approach the limit of his learning capacities because he must devote much of his adult life to earning a livelihood, rearing a family, and enjoying a little of noneducational life.

In plain fact, it is not enough that knowledge be good or useful; it also must be worth the cost. The argument for universal knowledge is no more sensible than an admonition to young students to memorize seven-place tables of logarithms or to learn to speak all languages fluently.

Men must learn some things in common, such as a language, a mathematics, and a logic, so that they can communicate with each other and peruse the parchments left by dead and distant men. They must also individually learn a small set of subjects tolerably well, in order to earn a livelihood. These are the necessities of social and economic life. It is helpful to know more; for example, a knowledge of a second language opens up a wider range of communication which may be useful to a professor, as well as to a door-to-door peddler.

So man cannot afford to learn all knowledge, or all social sciences, or economics, or even everything in one branch of economics. He must learn a trifling smattering of physics—enough to get out of the way of heavy falling objects—but need not have even a suspicion of the nature of genetics or Russian grammar or architecture.

He may be the loser if he spends his time reading trash instead of fine literature, or attending ball games instead of chamber music recitals, but he will survive well enough.

Each day of his life a man will need specialized knowledge of various sorts: how to deal with an infected cut; how to buy a house; how to start a balky automobile; how to fly a plane. These needs will ultimately be met by complicated pieces of knowledge, but it is sufficient to hire the specialists who possess this knowledge. The sore thumb may be cured by a new, extraordinarily complex antibiotic, but the patient need not even know its name; and, for that matter, the physician who prescribes it need not have the faintest idea of how to make the antibiotic. So long as every piece of specialized knowledge is known by someone, it is ultimately at the disposal of the high school dropout, although he is less likely to get it when needed than the college graduate.

Let us start over again: Why should people be economically literate, rather than musically literate, or historically literate, or chemically literate? If we are to give economics some special position, and ask that most people learn at least a modicum of economics, it must accordingly fall into one of two classes of knowledge: (1) as a means of communication among people, incorporating a basic vocabulary or logic that is so frequently encountered that the knowledge should be possessed by everyone; (2) as a type of knowledge frequently needed and yet not susceptible to economical purchase from experts. If economics does not meet one of these criteria, it has no special status relative to a hundred other disciplines. It may still be a most useful and even admirable branch of

knowledge, but that will be no justification for com-
manding every high school senior to study it.

The Pervasiveness of Economic Logic

Does economics meet the first criterion? Is it part of the
knowledge that is pervasive in communication and social
relationships? Yes, there is indeed a special economic
logic, and this logic is appropriately used in numerous
and highly diverse situations. This special economic logic
addresses itself to one problem: What arrangement of
one's limited means will lead to the most complete ful-
fillment of one's goals? The answer is loosely this: a resource should be diverted from less important to more
important uses—the principle of alternative costs. The
marginal importance of any use of a resource declines as
more resources are devoted to it—the principle of diminishing demand price. These principles are integral to all
rational behavior, and they work in ways so subtle that
their comprehension cannot be left to intuition or general
training in other disciplines. Bold claims! I shall try to
make the claims plausible.

Many thousands of people are killed each year in automobile accidents, and various groups are very active in
seeking to reduce these accidents by more rigorous examination of drivers and automobiles, more safely constructed automobiles and highways, lower speed limits,
and so on. Economic logic does not tell us what to do, but
it teaches us to look for the nonobvious costs and benefits of various policies. Here are a few of many possible
examples:

1. Lower speed limits reduce the value of the automobile to the user even as they lower the accident rate. If cars were sold with speed governors, the price one would pay on the average for a car with an 80-mile-per-hour limit might be $300 more than the price offered for a 60-mile-per-hour limit. Just because these prices are not quoted explicitly is no reason to ignore the value of speed. A good economist could make useful numerical estimates of the value of speed from auto prices or toll road usage.

2. It is an iron-clad rule, which most noneconomists deny most of the time, that the stiffer the price, the smaller the quantity purchased. Thus, apropos of whether liability for accidents would make a driver more careful, a substantial number of people would say that it would not, because the risk of injury or property damage to the person himself, plus the risk of arrest and perhaps loss of license, has all the deterrent effect to reckless driving that we can contrive. Liability for damages to others will buy no more care. This position, the economist can say with essential certainty, is simply wrong. How much *more* carefully people will drive when they have liability in addition to the other deterrents is another question—and one that, with study, we could answer.

3. The prohibition of driving by accident-prone drivers is often proposed and invoked, even when the drivers have resources sufficient to compensate anyone injured for the amount of the injury. I shall not seek to defend my belief that this is undesirable, but one aspect may be discussed usefully. Many people say that no value can be set upon a human life—no amount of compensation,

however vast, would compensate for a man's life. This is simply untrue so far as any sensible man is concerned: it depends upon the price. Men will drive trucks loaded with TNT at a sufficient wage, even though occasionally a truck and its driver are atomized. I will, and in fact do, fly on airplanes which could be safer if more were spent upon their construction, maintenance, and landing facilities, but I would rather crash once each 500,000 takeoffs than pay $900 for a trip from Chicago to New York and crash once every 3 million takeoffs. Furthermore, the community acting through the state behaves similarly: it does not build those railroad overpasses which would save one life per century or per thousand years; nor does it spend the extra thousand dollars on improved medical care which would save a life each decade. One must resist the temptation to regard such calculations as cruel or inhumane, because their purpose is the very opposite: their purpose is to assist in thinking about efficient ways to save human lives.

The problem of automobile safety could profitably occupy us much longer, but the above samples of the economic approach may suggest its utility.

The pervasiveness of economic logic may be illustrated further by the recent development of two new subjects. The first is *operations research,* in which quantitative method are used to determine the efficient solution of problems of business, education, military operations, and what not. A typical tool is the theory of queues, which allows us to plan the capacity of an operation so that it will not be wastefully large or, on the other hand, impose excessive costs of delay upon the user. Queues are involved in determining a community's need for hospital beds or a military airfield's repair facilities. The basic logic of operations research is that of traditional economic theory.

The second recently developed field is *decision theory.* Mathematical statisticians have developed powerful and versatile methods of making decisions under conditions of uncertainty, and again the basic logic is that of economics. Here, too, the role of economics is not fortuitous: it is the science of efficient purposive action.

So economics has a logic that is sufficiently pervasive to merit inclusion in the category of universal knowledge; unfortunately, it does not meet the condition of reasonable cost. This basic economic logic is taught only in advanced courses, and often unintentionally. Elementary textbooks make no effort to teach the logic of rational choice; they present the elements but do not show their depth or fecundity or universality. Nor can nonprofessional economists easily remedy the textbook deficiencies: it proves to be much easier to master either the geometry of price determination or the institutional details of the Federal Reserve System than the logic of economics.

So far as the first criterion goes, therefore, I would argue that economics belongs in everyone's education once we have learned how to teach it. The teaching of a subject is much more than putting one's mind to its elucidation. Arithmetic was much harder to learn with Roman numerals than after Arabic notation was adopted. That economic logic is not easily learned may be demonstrated by a fact that will surprise you: many highly intelligent, highly trained professors of economics have only a remote or formal knowledge of economic logic, *not* as a theoretical construct but as a constantly applicable and deeply illuminating principle. In fact, the Ph.D.'s from several celebrated centers are noted for both their technical facility and their inability to think like economists. Economics is not yet ready to be made a part of the basic curriculum of all educated men.

The Need for Do-It-Yourself Economic Analysis

And now the second criterion: Is economic knowledge frequently needed by the citizen but not readily purchased from experts? The individual citizen feels called upon to have an attitude toward most major pieces of legislation, and a good deal of this legislation is explicitly economic. All legislation affecting trade, employment, prices, or wages is predominantly economic in purpose. Much legislation devoted to other subjects—social policies, education, urban renewal, crime, product safety—has large economic effects. It seems obvious that a citizen would be assisted in forming intelligent opinions on this flood of legislation if he had some knowledge of economics.

Experts do not fully meet the citizen's needs for economic knowledge for two reasons. First, economic issues often involve the nature of fundamental social goals rather than technical economic knowledge. There is a dispute, perhaps, over whether farmers need aid, or whether cities should subsidize housing, or whether an inner-city area should be renewed. No expert can really answer such questions, although he could give the facts on farm income, low-income housing, or urban deterioration. Most experts operate more at the level of

technique: once the city decides to fluoridate the water—
which is partly a technical, medical question—the task is
completely turned over to the experts. Economists believe that economics helps clarify the nature of goals, but
the citizens who master economics will—like economists—be divided on goals.

Second, the expert advice on economic issues that does
come forth in ample quantity is often partisan. The industry presents its case, perhaps the regulatory commission presents *its* case, but no one presents a dispassionate
appraisal. Indeed, we do not even know how to define
dispassionate analysis. We certainly cannot say that professors of economics are objective, if for no other reason
than that they can hardly ever bring themselves to agree
upon a single position. The American Economic Association once created several committees to give consensus
reports on matters of public policy. They chose as their
first topic the Webb-Pomerene Act, which allows companies to combine in restraint of trade, provided they restrict their monopolistic plucking to the traditionally
proper geese—namely, foreigners. This law was probably
chosen as one on which there was only one valid side—
namely, opposition. The committee reached the conclusion that no conclusion could be reached.

So it would appear that every American must be his
own economist. Often matters of taste rather than of technical analysis are involved; and there is much partisan
professional advice, frequently hired by each party.

I have perhaps just demonstrated that economists are
untrustworthy, because of course these characteristics of
economic issues are not different from those in medicine
or engineering or sociology or other fields. Disputes over
goals enter into all public policies; and prejudice, interest,

and ideology enter the advice of physicists and physicians, as well as of economists. If one starts to read about a missile defense system or a public health program, for example, one soon discovers that there are numerous value judgments on which the experts have no expertise, and that there is a very substantial divergence of views among the experts on the most efficient policy to pursue. At a very specific level the experts may agree—for example, that it takes eight inches of concrete to bear a certain load, but at that level of specificity all the respectable economists also agree.

It appears, then, that the public has no *special* need for economic literacy. Economic issues are encountered much more often than (say) educational issues, but I suspect that this is simply because the public chooses to discuss economic issues more often. When one considers the prevalence of problems concerned with crime, family structure, and social relations, one can surely make at least as good a case for universal sociological literacy as for universal economic literacy. One could escape from this comparison by saying that economics as a discipline is more fully developed than sociology and that therefore economics can solve more of its problems. This is true, but I doubt whether the public at large shows this exquisite insight.

Yet this last point—that the public does concern itself most frequently with economic questions—is a true and persuasive reason for its possessing economic literacy. In the best of all worlds it might be most desirable to have musical or theological literacy, but in ours the public wants to talk about money. Although the public cannot have universal literacy, this is no reason for possessing no special knowledge at all. The public has chosen to speak and vote on economic problems, so the only open question is how intelligently it speaks and votes.

The Economics of Noneconomists

To say it differently, the public will learn its economics from economists or from somebody else. Economics will be purveyed by the history courses in our schools whether it is or is not taught in economics courses, and the quality of this nonprofessional economics is simply deplorable. Let me give just a few examples, chosen from two of the most popular textbooks on American history.

The first economist-historian is Thomas A. Bailey. Consider the following samples of "economic analysis":

Mortgages engulfed homesteads at an alarming rate; by 1890 Nebraska alone reported more than 100,000 farms blanketed with mortgages.

A network of interconnecting pipe lines radiated out from each of the twelve Federal Reserve reservoirs, and these speeded the flow of currency and credit to the areas in most serious financial distress.

What caused the Great Depression? The basic explanation seems to have been overproduction by both farm and factory . . . The ability of the nation to produce goods had clearly outrun its capacity to consume them or pay for them. Too much income was going into the hands of a few wealthy people, who invested it in new factories and other agencies of production. Not enough was going into salaries and wages, where revitalizing purchasing power could be more quickly felt.[1]

1. *The American Pageant*, 2nd ed. (Boston: Little, Brown, 1962), pp. 581, 692, 820.

Nothing courteous can be said about such economic analysis.

Further examples, if they are needed, are provided by the numerous and famous authors of *The National Experience.* C. Vann Woodward observes that in the closing decades of the nineteenth century, "there was nothing but the urging of conscience and the weak protest of labor to keep employers from cutting costs at the expense of their workers."[2] It would be equally perceptive for an economist to write: "The South would never have lost the Civil War if its soldiers had shown more agility in dodging bullets." John Blum writes of the 1929 crash: "Some two years before the crash, the annual rate of increase of national investment (as contrasted to speculation) had started downward, not the least because corporations and their executives had diminished expectations for profits from an economy in which purchasing power could no longer keep pace with productivity."[3] That well-known New York economist, Arthur M. Schlesinger, Jr., provides a new theory of price levels: "After the election in November [1946], Truman abandoned all controls. The conservative assault on the OPA was, in the end, responsible for the largest price rise in a single year in all American history."[4] To paraphrase the remark about Hungarian friends: with historians such as these, everybody needs an economist.

2. John M. Blum et al., *The National Experience*, 2nd ed. (New York: Harcourt, Brace and World, 1968), p. 456.

3. Ibid., p. 661.

4. Ibid., p. 769.

The Difficult Task of Achieving
Economic Literacy

Having argued that there is a case for economic literacy, I turn to my final theme—that it is an exasperatingly difficult form of literacy to teach. I will propose the disheartening thought that the level of economic literacy, in the correct sense of "literacy," is not rising and may well be declining. I will then explore briefly some of the reasons economic literacy is so hard to achieve, if only to guide us in our efforts to improve it.

One is tempted to define "economic literacy" as the knowledge and opinions that the speaker himself possesses; but then "literacy" is merely a synonym for "wisdom." The authoritative definition of economic literacy is "knowledge of the theories that are held by the professional economists." Time will eventually reveal that some of these theories are wrong and all are incomplete, but at any one time there is a best scientific view, and this best view must be the basis for any appraisal of literacy.

Accepting this criterion, Table 1 gives an assortment of

Table 1. Incorrect economic policies.

Policy	Professed goal	Objection
1. Oil import quotas	Provide domestic supplies in case of war	1. Confer subsidy on quota holders
		2. Not needed for national defense

Table 1 (*continued*)

Policy	Professed goal	Objection
2. Minimum wage	Increases income of poorly paid workers	Leads to unemployment of low-efficiency workers
3. Usury laws	Protect necessitous borrowers from high charges	Reduce availability of credit to the needy
4. American farm program	Increases income of farmers	1. Leads to wasteful use of resources 2. Aids landlords but not tenants
5. Tariffs	Protect American industries	Lead to wasteful use of resources (i.e., lower the standard of living)
6. TV channel grants	Prevent signal interference and improve programs	1. Confer subsidy on license holders

Table 1 (*continued*)

Policy	Professed goal	Objection
		2. No effect upon programs
7. Rural electrification	Provides cheap electricity to rural areas	1. Involves larger, disguised subsidy 2. Primary goal reached long ago
8. Urban transportation	Provides economical mass transportation	1. Irrational rate structures 2. Inefficient media (especially private automobiles)
9. Motor trucking regulation	Provides orderly transportation and protects railroads	1. Wasteful use of resources 2. Railroads should not be protected from open competition

existing economic policies of which the majority of professional economists disapprove. The disapproval is based upon either the ineffectiveness of the policy in reaching its goal, or the propriety of the goal. The goals with which the economists disagree are proximate economic goals (such as protection of industries from competition), not ultimate social goals (such as freedom or humanitarianism). The list is a relatively short one, but the policies are of economic importance, and the list could be much longer. One may conclude that economic policy in America contains much illiteracy.

We could make a corresponding list for 1868 that would even include tariffs analogous to those listed in 1968, although the nation in 1868 was much less protectionist than it is today. I am reasonably confident that the 1868 list would be much shorter. The discrepancies between professional economic opinion and public policy are at least as numerous and important as they were a century ago, and probably more so.

The persistence of widespread economic illiteracy is rooted in three conditions of the world:

1. Literacy of any form of intellectually respectable knowledge is hard to master. It requires application, intelligence, and instruction, and few people are fully literate in *any* subject.

2. Economics has a spurious simplicity because its policies are discussed in a language of which the educated layman knows each of the words. If all discussions of economics had to be conducted algebraically—which is how they are predominantly carried on in the professional economic journals—it would be more difficult to be deluded into believing that one understood tolerably an analysis which one did not understand at all.

3. People are wishful, not to say romantic, in their desires, and they much prefer easy and direct solutions to their problems. If there are unemployed textile workers, then stop imports of textiles from Hong Kong. If there is discrimination against black workers, then pass a law compelling people to be color blind. It is this wishfulness that makes the public so susceptible to the propaganda of both illiterate reformers and self-serving special interests.

I do not despair of raising the economic literacy of the American public unless we fall prey to the superficial idea that all that is necessary is a course or two for every young American. We shall have to combine vast efforts and creative experimentations if we are to produce the first economically literate society in history.

17

Wealth, and Possibly Liberty

A person is better off the more he earns and the more things the earnings will purchase for him.

The amount he earns depends upon his endowment of resources and the arenas in which these resources may be employed. The minimum of earnings will be achieved when the individual possesses only one resource (his labor) and is permitted to devote it to only one calling (as in a pure caste system), and earnings in this calling are miserly. From this minimum of earnings, the person's options may rise as more uses of his resources, and higher rates of payment for their use, become available. The economist summarizes this domain of possible productive activities by the budget equation: *Potential Earnings* $= \Sigma r_i p_i$, where r_i is the amount of resource i available per period, and p_i is its price.

Here I question the distinction between wealth and liberty, of which much is made by important libertarians such as Hayek.

In general, the potential earnings of the individual will be higher the wider his range of options. He may well find it most productive to specialize—say, as a physician—but unless he is free to enter this (and other) occupations, he cannot exploit his most favorable opportunities. If by luck or inheritance he is admitted to a sheltered, highly paid occupation, then most other people must be excluded from this occupation; and, on average, earnings in the society will be smaller than with free choice (because it is a condition for maximum output that men of equal ability earn equal amounts). The range of occupational choices open to a person will be wider the better endowed and trained he is, and the richer the society in which he resides.

The second side of a person's welfare is the way in which he may dispose of his earnings. The wider the choice of goods he may buy, and the lower their prices, the greater the satisfaction to be derived from given earnings. The economist summarizes these options also with a budget equation: *Spendings* $= \Sigma c_i p_i$, where c_i is the quantity of commodity or service i, and p_i is its price.

In a world of voluntary transactions—that is, transactions free of coercion—the two budget equations must be equal: *Potential Earnings* $=$ *Spendings*, since every use of a dollar is included in the array of spendings. (Of course, resources may also be used in spendings; one use of one's time is in consumption activities.)

We cannot rigorously say that the larger the sum of earnings and spendings, the better off the individual is. One obvious qualification must be made for inflation, but we shall put it aside by assuming that the price level is steady. A second qualification is that the modes of expenditure (or of earning) may become less suited to the individual: if my money income is held constant but I am forbidden to drive a car, my welfare has been damaged. (This restraint could be viewed as a decline in the purchasing power of money; and if the price level is defined as one that holds utility constant, then indeed a larger sum of earnings or spendings implies an increase in welfare.) But so long as I am free to choose methods of earning and spending, increases in these sums imply widening domains of choice.

A wider domain of choice is another way of saying that a person has more freedom or liberty. From this viewpoint, one can properly say that even with the vast expansion of public controls over earning and spending in the United States since the Civil War, there has been an enormous expansion in the average individual's liberty. He has many more occupations to choose among, many more areas in which to work and live, and enormously more products and services to consume. It is genuine limitation of my liberty if I cannot build a house that covers more than a specified fraction of my lot (whose minimum size is also prescribed), or that does not comply with construction, plumbing, wiring, and numerous other restrictions. But even with these restrictions, my choice of housing is vastly wider than it would be if I had lived a hundred years ago. Economic progress has increased choice even in highly regulated societies.

F. A. Hayek—and innumerable others—will accept the historical accuracy of the foregoing statements about the rise of wealth of the average person in Western society. But he will argue emphatically that this enlargement of choice is not to be confused with a growth of liberty. Liberty is freedom from the coercion of other *men:* " 'Freedom' refers solely to a relation of men to other men, and the only infringement on it is coercion by men. This means, in particular, that the range of physical possibilities from which a person can choose at a given moment has no direct relevance to freedom."[1] The ability of a man to make his own plans of action, and to make them under conditions not manipulated by other men, is the essential component of liberty or freedom for the individual. Hayek explicitly deplores the confusion of liberty with wealth, and believes that the actions of the state to redistribute wealth should be blamed on this confusion.[2] This position raises two questions: Can we distinguish coercion by other men from other limitations on our choice? And what purpose is served by the distinction?

First, as to the possibility of the distinction, one can surely argue that many (all?) of the restrictions imposed upon our range of choices by wealth are in some measure the product of the behavior of other men.

1. If I cannot attend a symphony concert because there are not enough other demanders of a symphony orchestra in my community, my wealth has been reduced (in utility terms) by the behavior of others.
2. If other people have reduced their demand for symphony concerts because of taxation (not necessarily progressive) of income by the state, and this was no part of the intention of the passage of the tax law, have I lost liberty or only wealth?

1. F. A. Hayek, *The Constitution of Liberty* (Chicago: University of Chicago Press, 1960), p. 12.
2. Ibid., p. 17.

In the latter case, I mention the intention of the legislature because Hayek frequently makes the essential element of liberty the freedom from the "arbitrary will" of another person.[3]

3. The state allows divorce but requires a procedure that costs the divorcing couple X dollars. Is this a restraint on liberty or a wealth limitation? The state fines an overtime parker $6. Is this a wealth limitation? If the state rented the parking space for $6, would this represent a reduction of liberty?
4. When the state uses economic sanctions to get obedience to laws—a policy that Gary Becker persuasively argues should be quite general—is it curtailing liberty?

The phrase "whether or not I am my own master"[4] is not transparent in its relationship to the actions of others. I doubt whether any important action of my life is wholly independent of the behavior of others, in the sense that I would behave differently if I were placed in another society. The deliberateness of the influence of others ranges from explicit commands (I may not practice medicine) to a wholly adventitious and unintended influence (my fellow citizens grow their hair longer, and I am a languishing barber). Or was it entirely unintended? Since the state can coerce by the exclusive use of economic sanctions, suppose it always did: Would not wealth be the only restriction of my choices? The distinction between wealth and liberty is not easily drawn, and in fact the task has not been undertaken in convincing explicitness.

3. Ibid., p. 21.
4. Ibid., p. 17.

The purpose of a distinction between wealth and liberty is also elusive. Whether the state forbids me (by a rationing system) to use more than ten gallons of gasoline a week, or whether I am prevented from doing so by its high price (not including taxes) is of little direct significance to me: in either case my driving is limited by decisions (to ration or to buy gasoline) of my fellow citizens. Hayek says, "The courtier living in the lap of luxury but at the beck and call of his prince may be much less free than a poor peasant or artisan, less able to live his own life and to choose his own opportunities for usefulness."[5] But we have two alternative answers: *either* the courtier chose that calling, and he esteems the perquisites as outweighing the uncertain hours and tasks; *or* he did not choose the calling, and his wealth in proper utility terms is small.

One is tempted to infer from the difficulties we encounter in distinguishing liberty that liberty is the freedom from *unnecessary* or *undesirable* restrictions upon the behavior of the individual. Hayek—in our final quotation from this leading philosopher of liberty—says: "Coercion is evil precisely because it thus eliminates an individual as a thinking and valuing person and makes him a bare tool in the achievement of the ends of another."[6] The master-slave relationship which is invoked here is avoidable in a way that the twenty-four-hour limitation on a man's time is not. It is not necessarily more avoidable, if we may judge by the long history of slavery, than the limitations which were put upon our choices by the technology and productive capacities of an earlier age.

5. Ibid.
6. Ibid., p. 21.

At this point, I suspect, the complaint at my obtuseness will no longer be repressible: Is not the coercion of one person by another *immoral?* This is a path I shall not follow, simply because I deny the existence of a widely accepted, coherent moral code in which noncoercion is an irresistible corollary. The assertion of moral values, in the absence of such a code, is either a disguised expression of personal preferences or a refusal to continue the analysis of a problem.

To avoid a discussion of morals is not to make the matter of coercion a matter of irrelevance. The concept of wealth is both broad and specific: it is the wealth of individual men, as judged by themselves, which measures their capacity to choose. One may derive normative conclusions on public policy by recourse to this criterion of individual utility maximization: indeed, this is a major occupation of economists. There is even a presumption in this literature that coercion is utility-reducing: unless the individual is incompetent (meaning too different?), he will in general suffer a loss of utility from coercive acts.

That line of argument on public policy is much esteemed, but I challenge its fertility and power compared to the somewhat different criterion of *efficiency* (that is, wealth maximization). Let me ask of any proposed or actual policy: Will it increase the wealth of the individuals in a society? If it does, on balance it will increase the range of options available to the people in that society. The income distributional effects of the change in wealth, I assert, will be swamped by the change in aggregate wealth: no significant increase in the wealth of the (individuals in a) society will adversely affect any large fraction of the members of the society, as a quite general rule.

I share Hayek's opposition to a host of modern public policies. They certainly cannot be opposed effectively on moral grounds: the moral views of a large share of the population are highly congruent with these policies. Perhaps these policies cannot be effectively opposed on *any* ground, but surely that of efficiency offers more promise. If a policy is demonstrably inefficient in achieving its goals, the more efficient policy ought to be preferred by members of the society. Unless one attributes irrationality to a society, the only noncoercive method of changing public policy is to present one that is more efficient in achieving the desired goals of the society. It is immensely more difficult to prove that a school voucher plan will serve the community's goals better than our present public school system than it is to show how one system better suits one's own preferences (moral scheme?). Unless the superior efficiency of a policy is shown, the prospects of influencing a rational society are negligible. If the society is irrational (that is, if it does not seek to maximize its members' utilities), then the forces determining its ideology (moral code?) are the only possible source of influence over the society's policies—and knowledge of economic laws will have no relevance to that influence.

18

The Intellectual
and the Marketplace

The intellectual has never felt kindly toward the marketplace: to him it has always been a place of vulgar men and base motives. Whether this intellectual be an ancient Greek philosopher, who viewed economic life as an unpleasant necessity that should never be allowed to become obtrusive or dominant, or whether this intellectual be a modern man, who focuses his scorn on gadgets and Madison Avenue, the basic similarity of view has been pronounced.

Now you and I are "intellectuals," as this word is used. I am one automatically because I am a professor, and buy more books than golf clubs. You are intellectuals because you are in general well educated and because you would

---

I wrote this to persuade young intellectuals that we should reexamine the traditional hostility toward private enterprise. I suppose I should not be surprised that it has been more successful in reaffirming businessmen in their faith. This is not an undesirable effect, but a lecturer denouncing cannibalism naturally must view the applause of vegetarians as equivocal evidence of his eloquence.

rather be a United States senator or a Nobel laureate than head of the Mobil Corporation. The question I wish to pose is not whether intellectuals should love the market-place—even a professor of economics of outrageously conservative tendencies cannot bring himself to say that the chants of five auctioneers rival a Mozart quintet. The questions are rather: What don't intellectuals like about the marketplace? And are they sure that their attitudes are socially useful?

Let us begin by noticing that from certain important viewpoints one would have expected intellectuals to be very kindly disposed toward that system of private enterprise which I call the marketplace.

First, if I may introduce a practical consideration, intellectuals by and large have elevated tastes—they like to eat, dress, and live well, and especially to travel. Walton Hamilton once said that our customary salutation, "Good day," was a vestige of an agricultural society where people were asking for good weather, and he expected city dwellers eventually to greet each other with the phrase "Low prices." If Hamilton's theory is correct, intellectuals will eventually adopt the greeting "Fair Fulbright."

Since intellectuals are not inexpensive, no society, until the rise of the modern enterprise system, could afford many intellectuals. As a wild guess, full-time intellectuals numbered 200 in Athens in the extraordinary age of Pericles, or about one for every 1,500 of population; and at most times in later history, intellectuals fell far, far short of this proportion. Today there are at least one million in the United States (taking only a fraction of those who live by pen and tongue into account), or one for each 200 of population. At least four out of every five owe their pleasant lives to the great achievements of the market-place. Professors are much more beholden to Henry Ford than to the foundation that bears his name and spreads his assets.

Not only have the productive achievements of the marketplace supported a much enlarged intellectual class, but also the leaders of the marketplace have personally been strong supporters of intellectuals, and in particular those in the academic world. If one asks where, in the Western university world, the freedom of inquiry of professors has been most staunchly defended and energetically promoted, my answer is this: not in the politically controlled universities, whether in the United States or Germany—legislatures are not overpopulated with tolerant men indifferent to popularity; and not in the self-perpetuating faculties, such as Oxford and Cambridge from 1700 to 1850—even intellectuals can become convinced that they have acquired ultimate truth, and that it can be preserved indefinitely by airing it before students once a year. No, inquiry has been most free in the college whose trustees are a group of top-quality leaders of the marketplace, men who, experience shows, are remarkably tolerant of almost everything except a mediocre and complacent faculty. Economics provides many examples: if a professor wishes to denounce aspects of big business, as I have, he will be wise to locate in a school whose trustees are big businessmen, and I have.

But debts are seldom the basis of friendship, and there is a much more powerful reason the intellectual might be sympathetic to the marketplace: the organizing principles of both areas are the same.

An enterprise system is a system of voluntary contract.

Neither fraud nor coercion is within the ethics of the market system. Indeed, there is no possibility of coercion in a pure enterprise system because the competition of rivals provides alternatives to every buyer or seller. All real economic systems contain some monopoly, and hence some coercive power for particular individuals; but the amount and the extent of such monopoly power are usually much exaggerated, and in any case monopoly is not an integral part of the logic of the system.

The intellectual world, and I speak chiefly but not exclusively of scholarship, is also a voluntary system. Its central credo is that opinions are to be formed from free discussion on the basis of full disclosure of evidence. Fraud and coercion are equally repugnant to the scholar. Freedom of thought is preserved by the open competition of scholars and ideas. Authority, the equivalent of monopoly power, is the great enemy of freedom of inquiry. Competition in scholarship is in some ways more violent than in business: the law sets limits on the disparagement of a rival's product, unless it is done in a book review in a learned journal.

Just as real markets have some fraud and monopoly, which impair the claims for the marketplace, so the intellectual world has its instances of coercion and deception, with the coercion exercised by claques and fashion. But again these deviants are outside the logic of the system.

Both areas, moreover, are democratic. The intellectual believes that every able and willing young person should get a good education whatever his race or financial background. The market believes that every able and willing person should be permitted to enter an industry or occupation, whatever his race or educational background.

There is food for thought in the fact that racial discrimination has diminished earlier, faster, and more quietly in the marketplace than in political life.

The analogies could be pursued much further, although not without danger of alienating all professors and most businessmen. I shall therefore merely mention, in passing, that both fields pay a fair amount of attention to packaging and advertising, and both fields place an absurdly high value on originality. There are also many minor differences, such as that the intellectual has no desire to know the marketplace, whereas the businessman wishes, or at least believes he wishes, to know the world of the intellectual. The basic fact is that the intellectual believes in the free market in ideas and, what is not quite the same thing, in words.

Yet whatever the latent sympathies of the intellectual for the marketplace, the hostilities are overt. The contempt for the "profit motive" which directs economic activity is widespread, and the suspicion of the behavior to which it leads is deep-seated. The charge that American society is materialistic has been recited more often than the Declaration of Independence, and has been translated into more foreign languages.

In one basic respect I believe that criticism by intellectuals is misplaced, and at times even hypocritical. The American economy produces many goods that are vulgar, silly, or meretricious, as judged by standards that I share with many intellectuals. It seems only proper to cite a few examples, if only to show how selective these standards are. I shall not propose the currently most popular item, the large and powerful automobile, because I have observed that it is mostly intellectuals of short stature who criticize such cars. But other examples are at hand. I am dissatisfied with the tastes of the nine-tenths of the population who believe that nonfictional books are to be read only by young people working for their B.A. I am dissatisfied with a population whose love for interesting music is so narrow that every symphony orchestra requires subsidies. I consider it shocking that more Americans have read *The Affluent Society* than *The Wealth of Nations*.

At the risk of appearing reasonable, I wish to qualify this complaint by observing that the tastes of the American public are more elevated than those of any other large society in history. Most societies have been judged by their cultural aristocracies—indeed, in earlier periods the vast majority of the population was not even considered to be a part of the culture of the society, for this vast majority was illiterate, tradition-bound, and lived for the most part brutishly in crude huts. Our society's tastes are judged by those of the vast majority of the population, and this majority today is generous, uncomplacent, and hard-working, with unprecedentedly large numbers engaged in further self-education, or in eager patronage of the arts. Our market-supported legitimate theater, which is surely the best in the world, is a suggestive measure of popular tastes.

These qualifications are not intended to withdraw the charge that the public's tastes should be better, and, for that matter, that the intellectual's tastes should be better. It is in fact a basic function of the intellectual to define the standards of good taste more clearly, and to persuade people to approach them more closely. It is proper to denounce vulgarity of taste, and to denounce it more strongly the more popular it is. It is permissible to reject certain desires completely—as we do when by compulsory education laws we reject the desire for illiteracy—although there is a strong presumption against the use of force in the area of tastes.

When I say that the complaints of deficiencies in tastes are misplaced when they are directed to the marketplace, I mean just that. The marketplace responds to the tastes of consumers with the goods and services that are salable, whether the tastes are elevated or depraved. It is unfair to criticize the marketplace for fulfilling these desires, when clearly the defects lie in the popular tastes themselves. I consider it a cowardly concession to a false extension of the idea of democracy to make *sub rosa* attacks on public tastes by denouncing the people who serve them. It is like blaming the waiters in restaurants for obesity.

To escape this response, the more sophisticated intellectuals have argued that people are told what to want by the marketplace—that advertising skillfully depraves and distorts popular desires. There is no doubt an element of truth in this response, but it is an element of trifling size. The advertising industry has no sovereign power to bend men's will—we are not children who blindly follow the last announcer's instructions to rush to the store for soap. Moreover, advertising itself is a completely neutral instrument, and lends itself to the dissemination of highly contradictory desires. While the automobile industry tells us not to drink while driving, the bourbon industry tells us not to drive while drinking. The symphony orchestra advertises, and gets much free publicity, in its rivalry with the rock band. Our colleges use every form of advertising, and indeed the typical university catalogue

would never stop Diogenes in his search for an honest
man.

So I believe that intellectuals would gain in candor and
in grace if they preached directly to the public instead of
using advertising as a whipping boy. I believe that they
would gain also in virtue if they would examine their own
tastes more critically: when a good comedian and a production of Hamlet are on rival channels, I wish I could be
confident that less than half the professors were laughing.

The main indictment of the intellectual, however, is
that the marketplace operates on the principle of self-
interest, and in fact, through competition, compels even
the philanthropic businessman to become self-serving.
Self-interest, often described with such neutral terms as
"egotism," "greed," and "dog-eat-dog," is viewed as a
crass, antisocial element of man's character, and an economic system that rests upon, and inculcates, this motive
achieves little admiration. In fact, a dislike for profit
seeking is one of the few specific attitudes shared by the
major religions.

I, too, find naked selfishness an unendearing trait, but I
have trouble separating it from the more admirable motives related to it. A prudent regard for one's own sur-
vival is generally applauded, even if the individual does
not say, "I got out of the way of the oncoming train only
to spare my Sunday School class pain." The violent endeavors of an athlete to defeat his rivals are much admired, providing the contest is more or less fair, even
though the winner is expected not to say, "I'm glad I
won—chiefly because I'm vain, but secondarily for the
honor of Sheboygan High School."

Even in fields somewhat removed from the athletic

arena, the roles of self-interest and what for lack of a better name I shall call "benevolence" are perplexingly interwoven. I have spent my life among college teachers, although admittedly in the most competitive branch of research and publication. In one sense the disinterest of my colleagues is beyond doubt: I have seen silly people—public officials as well as private—try to buy opinions, but I have not seen or even suspected any cases in which any important economist sold his professional convictions. It is also true that many of the best professors could earn more in other callings.

But on the other hand, the motives that drive economists are not completely clear, either. When they strive to solve a scientific problem, is ambition for their own professional status completely overshadowed by love of knowledge? I wonder. When they write an article to demonstrate the fallacies of someone else's work, is their hatred for error never mixed with a tiny bit of glee at the display of their own cleverness? I wonder.

To shift elsewhere, I have never encountered a political candidate who said, "I am running for office because I, with my dear spouse and future administrative assistant, can earn more in politics than elsewhere." Nor do I expect to. But the language of public interest surely covers a good many acres of self-interest.

A major source of the view that the marketplace places special values on self-interest, beyond those more or less evident in all human behavior, is the belief that one man's gain is another's loss, that business, like the so-called friendly poker session, is a zero-sum game. Not so.

On the one hand, it must be recognized that the great source of market gains is the productivity of the participants. Unlike the poker game, the wealth of our society has been doubling even on a per capita basis every twenty-five years, and the doubling has been due to the labors and ingenuity of the men in the marketplace. Of course, there are also incomes achieved by monopoly rather than by efficiency, by fraud rather than by output; but it would be a wholly extravagant estimate that they amount to 10 percent of the income of the marketplace. There is room for improvement here, but there is vastly more room to admire the prodigious production achievements of the marketplace.

On the other hand, I would emphasize that most of the gains from innovation in the marketplace are passed on to the community at large. A new idea may yield handsome profits for a time, but the rapid rush of competition soon drives the price of the product down to a modest level. Ballpoint pens were first marketed at $12.50 to those penmen eager to write underwater (and, judging by my experience, only underwater); they rapidly fell in price and, as you know, are now so cheap that you have no economic excuse if you do not write the Great American Novel. Sears, Roebuck and Company and Montgomery Ward made a good deal of money in the process of improving our rural marketing structure, but I am convinced that they did more for the poor farmers of America than the sum total of the federal agricultural support programs of the last five decades.

It is an interesting illustration of the great influence of the intellectual that the marketplace itself has become apologetic of its pursuit of profit. The captains of industry now list, in a world in which public relations are becoming as important as efficiency, among their major achievements the great number of bowling alleys or college fellowships they have given to their employees. To boast that large profits demonstrate great efficiency in producing existing products and introducing new ones is considered even by them to be too archaic a form of thought for public consumption. The patron saint of economics, Adam Smith, once wrote: "I have never known much good done by those who affected to trade for the public good. It is an affectation, indeed, not very common among merchants, and very few words need be employed in dissuading them from it." I wonder what those very few words were.

To return to intellectuals, their dislike for the profit motive of the marketplace no doubt rests in part on a failure to understand its logic and workings. It is a fact painful to record that the level of economic literacy has not risen noticeably in the twentieth century. Indeed, as professional economics becomes more complicated and its practitioners use an increasingly more formidable apparatus, there seems to have been retrogression in the ability of economists to communicate with other intellectuals. Less than a century ago a treatise on economics began with a sentence such as, "Economics is a study of mankind in the ordinary business of life." Today it will often begin, "This unavoidably lengthy treatise is devoted to an examination of an economy in which the second derivatives of the utility function possess a finite number of discontinuities. To keep the problem manageable, I assume that each individual consumes only two goods, and dies after one Robertsonian week. Only elementary mathematical tools such as topology will be employed, incessantly."

But misunderstanding is not the whole explanation: I cannot believe that any amount of economic training would wholly eliminate the instinctive dislike for a system of organizing economic life through the search for profits. It will still appear to many intellectuals that a system in which men were driven by a reasonably selfless devotion to the welfare of other men would be superior to one in which they sought their own preferment. This ethic is deeply embedded in the major religions.

I personally also believe that the good society will be populated by people who place a great value on other people's welfare. This is, however, not the only attribute of the good society; in particular, in the good society a man should be free within the widest possible limits of other men's limitations on his beliefs and actions. This great ethic of individual freedom clashes with that of benevolence, for I can seldom do positive good to another person without limiting him. I can, it is true, simply give him money, but even in this extreme case where I seem to place no bonds on him, he inevitably faces the question of what conduct on his part will lead me to give money to him again. Usually I will find it hard to be content to do so little good—giving money to improve a man's food or housing or health will seem as inefficient as giving him gasoline so that he will drive more often to museums. Hence, when I give money I shall also insist that it be spent on housing, or on medical care for his children, or on growing wheat in the way that I think is socially desirable, or on the collected works of Burke and de Tocqueville, or of Marx and Lenin. A patron tends to be paternalistic—in a nice way, of course. I am not saying that benevolence is bad, but that like everything else it can be carried to excess.

One final question on motives: Why are they so important? Am I to admire a man who injures me in an awkward and mistaken attempt to protect me, and to despise a man who to earn a good income performs for me some great and lasting service? Oddly enough, I suspect an answer is that motive makes a difference—that it is less objectionable to be injured by an incompetent benefactor than by a competent villain. But I leave with you the question: Are motives as important as effects?

Several charges related to the dominance of self-interest have rounded out the intellectual's indictment of the marketplace. First, the system makes no provision for men whose talents and interests are not oriented to profit-seeking economic activity. Second, there are cumulative tendencies toward increasing inequality of wealth, which—if unchecked—will polarize the society into a great number of poor and a few very rich. Third, the game in the marketplace is unfair in that inheritance of property plays an immensely larger role in success than the efforts of the individuals themselves. I shall comment briefly on each of these assertions.

The first charge is true: the marketplace will not supply income to a man who will not supply something that people want. People have enormously varied desires, but not enough of them wish to hire men to engage in research on ancient languages nor, eighty years ago, did they hire men to study quantum mechanics. The marketplace does not provide an air force or alms for the poor. It does not even supply babies. I conclude that a society needs more than a marketplace.

The second charge, that there are cumulative tendencies to ever-increasing inequality of wealth, is untrue. I would indeed ignore the charge for fear of reprimand from the Society for the Prevention of Cruelty to Straw Men, were it not that this straw man is so popular. In plain historical fact, the inequality in the distribution of income has been diminishing, and the diminution has been due to market forces even more than to governmental efforts. It is also worth noting that a modern market economy has a less unequal income distribution than in either centrally directed or unindustrialized economies.

The third charge, that inheritance of property plays a dominant role in the distribution of income in the marketplace, is an overstatement. Inheritance of property is important, but it will give some perspective to the charge to notice that property income is only one-fifth of national income, and inherited property is less than half of all property; so less than 10 percent of all income is governed by inheritance of property.

No useful purpose would be served by trying to appraise the proper role of inheritance of property in a few passing remarks. We would have to look carefully at the effects of inheritance on incentives; we would have to look at gifts during life, which are almost equivalent to bequests; and we would have to decide whether privately endowed colleges do enough good to offset the inevitable high-living heirs.

But our greatest problem would be that inheritance extends far beyond a safe deposit box full of bonds and stocks. I have told you that you are intelligent; I now add that the chief reason you are intelligent is that your parents are intelligent. Some of you, especially the younger of you, may find this unbelievable: Mark Twain said he was astonished by how much his father had learned during the short time it took Twain himself to age from eighteen to twenty-one. But inheritance of ability is important, probably more important in its effects on the distribution of income than is the inheritance of property. So a full account of the proper role of inheritance would have to extend to ability, and perhaps even to name and reputation, as the senior senator from Massachusetts might agree. The social and legal institutions governing inheritance in our society are surely open to improvement, but we are unlikely to improve them if we are guided by nothing more than naive egalitarianism.

And now to my final point. Intellectuals are great believers in the human mind and in its ability to conquer an ever larger part of the immense domain of ignorance. But they have not made much use of the mind in reaching their views on the economic organization appropriate to the good society so far as its basic cultural values go. It is clear that the kinds of traits that are fostered in man are influenced by (but, of course, not only by) the way economic life is organized. After all, throughout history men have spent half their waking hours in economic activity.

Important as the moral influences of the marketplace are, they have not been subjected to any real study. The immense proliferation of general education, of scientific progress, and of democracy are all coincidental in time and place with the emergence of the free enterprise system of organizing the marketplace. I believe this coincidence was not accidental: the economic progress of the past three centuries was both cause and effect of this general growth of freedom. The dominant era of the free marketplace was the nineteenth century. I believe, but with less confidence, that the absence of major wars in that century—the only peaceable century in history—was related to this reign of liberty. I believe, again with less confidence, that the contemporary transformation of the British public from a violent and unruly people into a population of almost painful Victorian rectitude was related to this reign of liberty.

These beliefs may be right or wrong, but they are not matters of taste. They are hypotheses concerning the relationship between economic and social organization, and are subject to analytical development and empirical testing. It is time that we did so, high time. Our ruling attitude toward the marketplace has not changed since the time of Plato. Is it not possible that it is time to rethink the question?

Sources and Acknowledgments
Index

Sources and Acknowledgments

Chapter 1. Originally published in *Bulletin of the American Association of University Professors* 33 (Winter 1947): 661–665.

Chapter 2. Originally published in *Bulletin of the American Association of University Professors* 37 (Winter 1951–52): 650–656.

Chapter 3. Written in 1960; published for the first time in 1963, in the first edition of this book.

Chapter 4. Originally published in *Journal of Political Economy* 75 (February 1967): 100–101. Reprinted by permission of the publisher.

Chapter 5. Written in 1958 at the Center for Advanced Study in the Behavioral Sciences, Stanford, California. Published for the first time in 1963, in the first edition of this book.

Chapter 6. Published for the first time in 1963, in the first edition of this book.

Chapter 7. Originally published in *Journal of Political Economy* 85, no. 2 (1977): 441–443. Reprinted by permission of the publisher.

Chapter 8. Originally published in *Journal of Political Economy* 81, no. 2, pt. 1 (1973): 491–495. Reprinted by permission of the publisher.

Chapter 9. Originally presented in 1962, as a speech delivered at the annual trustees' dinner of the University of Chicago. Published for the first time in the first edition of this book.

Chapters 10–14. Published for the first time in 1963, in the first edition of this book.

Chapter 15. Originally published in *American Economic Review, Proceedings* 53 (May 1963): 653–659.

Chapter 16. Originally published in *Journal of Economic Education* 1 (Spring 1970): 77–84. A publication of the Helen Dwight Reid Educational Foundation. Reprinted by permission.

Chapter 17. Originally published in *Journal of Legal Studies* 7, no. 2 (1978): 213–217. Reprinted by permission of the publisher.

Chapter 18. Published for the first time in 1963, in the first edition of this book.

Index